Sell More and Have Happier Customers

Sally Roberts

Fun Training For Results Ltd

Copyright © 2023 Sally Roberts

All rights reserved

The characters and events portrayed in this book are fictitious. Any similarity to real persons, living or dead, is coincidental and not intended by the author.

No part of this book may be reproduced, stored in a retrieval system, or transmitted in any form or by any means, electronic, mechanical, photocopying, recording, or otherwise, without express written permission of the publisher.

ISBN: 9798854681148

Cover design by: Simon Glenn

INTRODUCTION

THE BEGINNING

A sales book entitled "How To Sell" has been on the list since Fun Training For Results began, nearly seven years ago. An interest in selling and how to do it, well that has been ongoing since a Saturday job at "Flowers by Jean" back in the 1980s. The florist's shop was on a high street in Horsforth and very 'Yorkshire'. The upsell opportunity was Chrysal, a little sachet of flower food at just 10p. The owner noted how many 10p upsells were added to each transaction. I was sixteen, selling flowers and upselling very well!

From floristry to electrical sales! I know, impressive! There was a paper round, car wash run and fast food in between, but I hit the big time at Comet! Out of this world, or so I thought at the time. A college work experience job on the shop floor at Comet led to a Saturday job there and as many free days as I could offer them. TVs, huge camcorders, washing machines, you name it, if you could plug it in, then Comet sold it. The upsell this time was the ever-debated, extended warranty. Imagine you go all out and buy the latest, exciting, multi-function, big load, high spin washing machine for a whopping £350 to then be invited to purchase additional insurance for about a further £100 in case it goes wrong! Looking back, it is staggering to think that anyone bought it, but they did. There was one occasion where I excelled and for the record, I am no longer proud of the achievement. The gentleman wanted a stereo, so I sold him, really sold him. A stereo made up of separates, amp, cassette, radio, record player, speakers the lot. After this hefty purchase for a state-of-the-art, cutting-edge sound system, rather than offering an extended warranty on the whole unit, I suggested he purchase a warranty on each part of the system. He did! I celebrated, and so did my manager, Stuart. The commission that month was extraordinary, the warranty target was hit by the store and the celebrations were huge. Did I do the right thing? Absolutely not!

Thirty-plus years later and I sincerely regret selling him something he did not need. It was wrong and when he did realise, I am quite sure he would never return to Comet or trust a salesperson ever again. So, if you are reading this, sir, I would like to offer my sincere apologies for being such a brash, naïve, insensitive, persuasive teenager and effectively conning you out of lots of money.

Maybe that is why writing this book is so important to me. I want to set straight that proper selling can look very different. Sincere selling is the opposite to a speedy, transactional, get as much dollar as you can as fast as you can and move on approach. That is not good, not right and, commercially very foolish.

Newspaper classifieds became the next step in a brilliant sales career, selling space! One minute you saw it - next it was used to wrap your fish 'n chips. (This was the '80s remember!) You are selling what might happen as a result of an advert. Let relationship building begin. Truly recognising the benefit of getting to know the person, people, or company that you are there to help. Understanding their vision and goals, their objectives and then creating solutions to make it all happen. One solution, the Bicester Bear, was a career highlight! Walking around Bicester to select loyal customers with said 6ft bear for a photo-op. The customers and readers loved it! The Bicester Buyers Guide that accompanied the bear was a sellout, made the dollar and became a template for other areas. It began because I listened to my customers.

Media took hold, moving from paper to magazine to national publications. The premise stayed the same - look after people, listen, create solutions and the dollar follows. I noted a serious lack of understanding of this simple notion, people first, always. Training, upskilling, and ensuring the highest standard were usually bypassed for a speedy sale, a quick buck and a target hit. Especially in the media world.

In the late 1980's a move into training. Working with hungry, really hungry salespeople was honestly a baptism of fire. I had talked my way into the job and 'Out of my depth,' was an understatement. Time to own it, jump in, have a go, begin the vertical learning curve, and deliver. So, I did! Talking at a room full of mostly media guys who wanted Porsches and drank Bollinger, entertained clients from midday Thursday to Friday, was a bad idea. I desperately needed a plan. If I were them, what would spark my desire to want to be in a training session? Music, (rave or disco preferably), incense burning, a picture of that Porsche? Let's move the chairs and dance, stand up, deliver a surprise, and get involved. This was training like they had never seen or experienced before. For that matter neither had I but it worked, backed up with coaching side by side and 121s. Somehow, we won the prestigious IIP, Investors In People, the Porsches were purchased and all targets were smashed.

Plan B delivered results. Was I winging it, flying by the seat of my pants? Hell, yes! Did it work? Thankfully, yes!

Training, Fun Training had begun!

By this point, I was the top sales biller in the UK for a large media company. I had sat through some seriously uninspired training and knew I could do better.

It was September 2016. Today the business looks nothing like it did then, but I began. Day courses were soon replaced with modules. Workshops were replaced with me going into the client's business, understanding the people and their roles, training, setting tasks and ensuring accountability and so creating immediate results. Every company I have worked with has smashed their targets. Every company I have worked with comes to understand the benefit of going all out to delight customers. They value the training experience and use it to deliver results. Being with people and training them to deliver extraordinary solutions that see their clients referring them is the best feeling. Recommendations from respected business leaders that praise the impact the training has had on their people, culture, and bottom line, that is the best feeling too!

Now the time is right to share the training more widely than is possible in person.

You will most likely be familiar with the question 'Which came first, the chicken or the egg? 'It ensures ongoing debate and to date I remain unsure if it was ever answered.

It is the same in business around selling. People, companies, and organisations say, "We want to sell more, to grow, and have more money in the till". Makes sense and sounds like a good idea. Next, they enrol on a sales course, watch a video, or buy a book all about selling. The book is read, the course completed, and the online module downloaded, but sadly success is not guaranteed. You see, to sell more you need to know more than how to sell. The skill of 'how to sell 'is the final part of being able to sell more.

To sell more you need to focus on three separate stages. In order these are attitude, opportunity creation and lastly a sales process.

A superb sales mindset, your attitude, is critical if you want to sell, put the money in the till and achieve growth. Attitude is a great starting point but now something else is needed. New opportunity to sell to. Unlike the chicken/egg analogy, this looks like chicken, egg and omelette. If the omelette is the sale, it cannot be made until you have the egg.

Put simply, in business, if you want to sell you have to have a great attitude and be able to find new opportunities before ultimately rolling out a proven sales process.

This book teaches just that. Comprised of three parts, it delves first into a selling mindset, looking at positivity, being efficient with time and not being a tree. Only when you have the right mindset can successful prospecting for opportunities begin. In the second part, all the tools in the prospecting toolbox are delivered and discussed. Which one will bring you a greater return? Finally, when the winning mindset has led to great prospecting and you're faced with an opportunity to sell, part three provides a proven sales process that acknowledges big sales take more time and effort. Its eleven steps ensure you will make a sale, put money in the till and achieve growth.

The three parts go hand in hand, one without the others and you have no omelette.

Unlike most sales and business books, you will find here a cast of businesspeople that you will recognise, characters you have come across and scenarios you will find relatable. The book is real and relevant and offers ideas, solutions, and suggestions on how to sell more and have happier customers. How you use it - that bit is in your domain.

Above all, have fun! Laugh as you read about how Wing It Wayne crashed and On It Olly excelled. Meet Toby, the cynic in the room. Throughout the book, he asks welcome questions that you might relate to.

Make it work by having a go, one step at a time. Stay in touch, and let me know how you get on, how happy your customers are and how you have surpassed your own and their expectations. Share your new skills and even more customers will be delighted.

Enjoy, learn, and use!

CONTENTS

Part 1: A Sales Mindset

Selling more begins with your mindset.

However great the product or service you are selling, regardless of the promotion, deal, or incentive to buy right now, your mindset will determine the outcome. Whichever slick sales trick you have learned or sales process you have ready to implement, it is all wasted if your mindset is out of sorts. Before any prospecting or selling comes the critical need to understand what a sales mindset looks like, why you need one and how to achieve yours.

Part One begins with the understanding that you drive your day. Being positive, feeding your brain healthy information and recognising your achievement matters. Parking excuses, knowing your priorities, and making time to sell come next. Then understand the power of the brain and how being liked is critical if wanting to sell more. Taking time to build relationships, having just a coffee, and ensuring your first impression with a big fish is fabulous. Listening to every word and responding with influential language wraps up part one.

1. You're Not A Tree
2. Positivity Matters - inc feed the brain
3. Achievement
4. Time
5. People Buy You
6. It's Just Coffee
7. A Fabulous First Impression
8. Say Less, Sell More

9. It's How You Say It

Part 2: Prospecting

Finding people to sell to.

There are many excellent courses, books and guides that share various processes of how to sell. Steps, stages, or a formula all promise sales at the end if used correctly. The big flaw in all these suggestions on how to sell is who to sell to. Being a master at an art, in this case selling, is wasted if you have no one to sell to.

Prospecting, hunting, business development - call it by any title, simply put, how are you going to find new opportunity, people to sell to and businesses that want what you have to offer.

Part 2 looks initially at how you maximise opportunities to sell more with your existing client base. Mindset returns with a closer look at the tenacious, gritty quality required if you are to succeed at quality, precision, efficient prospecting. Finally, prioritising time to prospect, understanding the need for consistency and then using all the tools in the prospecting toolbox to achieve your objective.

10. Before You Prospect, Maximise Opportunity
11. A Prospecting Mindset
12. Make Time to Prospect
13. The Prospecting Toolbox
14. Referrals
15. Networking
16. The Sales Call
17. The Voicemail
18. Email

19. Exhibition

20. Social Media

Part 3: The Sales Process

Time to sell, the calls to Ethel have paid off and this is it, you are in front of the decision-maker. Where many may launch into a full-on presentation, others run, panic, and go straight to money or worse, discount. The sales call is critical to future business growth and to blow it now would be a disaster. The good news is that by following a proven sales process you can sell successfully. Sometimes in one call, often in a few, remembering big fish go slow.

Part 3 breaks down the steps and discusses each in detail. Like learning to drive it might seem strange, odd and a bit awkward to begin with, then in time as you try, have a go, and create a habit, it will flow and become just what you do.

This sales process works and like learning any new skill it will take an investment of time. When you master the process and combine it with excellent prospecting and a winning mindset, the combination is exciting and will see you soar.

21. The Sales Process - Why?

22. Step 1 - Plan and Preparation

23. Step 2 - Intro and Empathy

24. Step 3 - Signpost

25. Step 4 - WHATSAS

26. Money Talks

27. Step 5 - The Gap

28. Step 6 - About The Pitch

29. Step 6a - Create a Pitch

30. Step 7 - Trail Close

31. Step 8 - Recommend

32. Step 9 - Close

33. Step 10 - Consolidate

34. Step 11 - Referral

Summary - Make It Live

About The Author

Character List

PART 1

MINDSET

1 You're Not a Tree!

Please stand up and be a tree! The request is usually made on the first training session and is met with curious looks. Toby would say "Really, a tree?"

When standing as a group, being trees and often throwing in some beautiful tree shapes, I suggest to them that they are not trees. At this point, Toby would say calmly, "We are not trees, Sally".

Exactly, point made, although usually it takes a while to land. You are not a tree. You are a fully-fledged human being in good health and of sound mind. That is why you are at work doing what you do.

When it lands that you're not a tree and the understanding follows that you are responsible for driving your day, then wow! That moment is incredible.

You see, being a tree is how many of us like to spend our time. Much easier to hand over the decision-making, autonomy, and power to someone else, to negate responsibility for our own life. It's easier to blame, to look away, put our head in the sand or under the duvet, to ignore, run and do anything other than acknowledge we are responsible for our day. You are definitely not a tree!

It is massive really. I ask if anyone's mum dropped them at work, coerced them to go in and then watched from the gates to ensure they stayed doing their job. Were they picked up at 5 pm, taken home and told what they were having for tea? Laughter follows and 'Of course not'. Then a quick check that when they came to work that morning, they put their feet into the building, they drove themselves to work, and they chose to be there on time or not. Simply, you choose to come to work because, (has it landed yet?), you're not a tree.

Accountability.

This can take time, but when you stop blaming and take on board that today is yours - Wow! You could be unstoppable! Then you recognise that the next 24 hours can be lived exactly as you choose and expectations can be surpassed. Then you realise that you have the power to make the things happen that you want to happen. Incredible!

Many people don't take ownership of their day and that's OK. If you're happy, content and living your best life without ambition and a desire to do more or make a difference, then stay in that place. Just be you. If, however, you are that person who wants more yet looks to blame others, (circumstances, weather, the economy) for how all these things are preventing you, well maybe it's time you understood you're not a tree.

When working with a company who were choosing their values, accountability was viewed as a good one to include. It was discussed, the definition debated and all agreed, to 'Own It!'

They signed up for the responsibility to make things right when they make a mistake, admit when they are wrong, and see that all tasks are done well and to completion. To "Own it." The response was enthusiastic, positive, and understood, in the training room at least.

Moments later there was a conversation about an event that had not happened, and blame shot out of a person's mouth in a matter of seconds. Then there was confusion as to why something remained undelivered, followed by more blame. Apparently, a rep was late in getting to an appointment. The rep blamed the traffic, the weather and the alarm clock for not going off.

It is so easy to lay blame at another's door, any door rather than face the situation head-on and acknowledge that 'you drive you'. There will always be weather, traffic and unhappy customers so looking to place blame for what you did not do is unhelpful.

When people have autonomy, (are not trees), sales growth accelerates, culture is improved, and trust is built.

When you are trusted, given autonomy to make mistakes and learn from them, to create innovative ideas and share your knowledge without fear of reprimand or rebuff or a downright "No", then the results can be amazing. (We cover No and Language in a future chapter.)

When people are micromanaged with all decisions made by the MD and innovative ideas are met with blockers, then people can become trees in your business and that is unhealthy.

Quashing people who bring brilliance, innovation and ambition to a role is sad.

Trees don't go the extra mile - they are stuck.

Toby speaks up, "How do we not be a tree in a sales role? Everyone knows what to do in sales?"

It begins with attitude. Usually, at this point, I ask teams to draw a blender. The pictures vary and some are super slick, from a Kenwood to a Magi Mix!

Into the blender go three ingredients required for a great attitude, a must-have if you are to have a sales mindset:
- Owning it, understanding that you are responsible for you subjective responsibility, not being a tree! It is a good place to start. You can't make or dictate how other people see their life, but you can choose for yourself.
- Next is graft, grit, and hard work, understanding that nothing, absolutely nothing comes for free. Also, life is not perfect or fair but when you work hard you can create results. Doing nothing will get you nothing.

Toby laughs, "Yes, but you can do the lottery."
- Yes, you can Toby, good luck!

I ask if anyone has been to the ballet, a concert recently or a football match, how was it? The enthusiastic reply is that they were brilliant, sensational, top of their game. They were all those things because they worked hard. They did not just become a Boom, Wow, Sensation! - it took years, practising a pirouette, a series of notes, or a side pass. We are so excited by fast and easy that often we are led to believe that fame, talent, or skill just appears one day without effort. It doesn't! It takes grit, commitment, and graft - real graft.
Think Tom Daley and diving. He didn't just get gold, albeit that is the moment we celebrate, go wild for. We say he is so talented, a natural. Rarely do we look at the back story, the 4 am starts from an early age, passing up wild nights out to practice and continuous up and down to the diving board on repeat for years. That is way less "Ye hah" than, "He's so talented." He is so talented because he backed it up with sheer graft. Nothing comes for free. Work hard at what you want if you are to have any chance of making it happen.

Sit back, put your feet up and do nothing. You will be rewarded with nothing.

The next ingredient goes into the blender:
- Just be you.

Toby glances, "Be You?"
- Yes, Toby, be you, be who you truly want to be. Are you striving to be kind, helpful and to delight? Then do that. Are you keen to be trusted? Then go all out to build trust. Be the person you want to be. After all, we have one shot at this life thing, so make it count. Think of the iconic Nelson Mandela. He was who he wanted to be to the point of being imprisoned. He was true to himself. James Timpson who now owns the shoe repair chain is true to himself and does business differently. Why bother with a

CV? If we like and trust you, you are in. He and his company help people, not just a charitable donation and a trophy at an awards gala to look good. He helps, offering jobs, perks, support, and holidays.

Being true to yourself matters. If you are watching Wolfe on Wall Street and thinking sales and business are super slick, tricks and dollar then you have got it wrong. Pretending to be someone you are not because you think that is what is required to sell, will catch you out. Being authentic and being true to yourself works, with all your quirks, hobbies, and passions. To be trusted and have integrity takes time and effort, beginning a relationship with the real you is a good starting point.

Early on in business, I was given the opportunity to sign some legal papers to enable funding for a client to pay me. It was in theory just a signature and a bit of paper. Many do sign, take the dollar, and move on. I didn't. No bells and whistles, it just felt, the emotional thing again, wrong. To sign to say that training would look a certain way when it wouldn't felt wrong, dishonest, and fake. I chose honesty over dollar and that integrity stays way longer than a training contract. Walking away from people and business that does not sit right with you and your vision is OK. Be who you want to be and be around people who inspire and support you to be that person or business.

To have a great attitude, a key element of a sales mindset, you need to mix up owning it, graft and being authentic. Some days you will work harder than others. On occasions, you might want to hide and take time out to think.

Add owning it, graft and integrity to your life blender, then press "go." A mix of all these ingredients will enable a great attitude, necessary to be an excellent sales superstar.

Doing all that is a brilliant starting point for delighting clients, nurturing relationships, and guess what? Do all that and the sales will follow.

2 Positivity Matters!

Do you recall the miserable sales assistant that could barely raise her head to look at you, let alone serve you? Or recall the time a salesperson came to visit and spent the whole time talking about themselves and how rubbish everything around them was? Or the work colleague who only ever calls to despair and complain about pretty much everything?

Mmmm, funny that! Being positive sits next to attitude. It is something that you must choose to do, to be intentional about being positive. Worth repeating each day, if you want to be positive, it is your decision.

Given that positive salespeople sell about 37% more than miserable ones (Martin Seligman), it's worthwhile embracing positivity.

"How?" asks Toby, all serious in his question. "How do you be positive? It's just not that easy." Toby is right. There can be days or moments when looking for and finding a silver lining is tricky but mostly if you're reading this, then you have good reason to be positive.

Let's begin with gratitude. Every morning before 6 am I head off for a walk, leaving my house and going down the first ginnel, the gratitude ginnel. Ok, so if you're not from Yorkshire you might not know what a ginnel is. It's an alley, a narrow path between the houses, a shortcut, a ginnel. I call this one my gratitude ginnel. I begin by saying thank you for three things from the day before. Sometimes it might be a delicious pizza without cheese and added anchovies, a chic flick and a great sleep or it might be a huge thing, like winning a new account, a beautiful event or, spending time with family. Either way, each day begins with gratitude, saying thank you to The Universe, God, Buddha, whoever. Recognising good things and giving thanks sets up the day positively.

Companies that live a culture of positivity and saying thanks have a higher positivity quota and they sell more. One time in training, a young lady who had enjoyed a pretty rough weekend looked at me despairingly and said, "Really, Sally, you want me to be grateful - for what?"

She is a great person and on this occasion, she was wallowing big time. I asked if she had turned on the tap that morning.
"Of course, to make coffee. I needed coffee."
- Ok so what came out of the tap?
"Well, water, dah!"
- So, you have clean water from a tap and good coffee?
"Yes."
- Well, that is a good beginning to being grateful. Then a quick check,
- Were you mugged on your way to work, were you walking through a war zone or scared of being kidnapped?
"No, Sally and, yes, OK, I get you!"

It is easy to focus on what we do not have. To look out for all the things that are wrong in life. Scarily if we then dwell on them, talk about them, share them, pick them apart and give them even more attention, they grow. If we email, text and post on social media about the negative stuff, guess what? It gets bigger and you become responsible for sending negativity to others. In a day with 24 hours of opportunity to be positive, when living in a safe place with, running water as a starter, then being grateful is possible and it matters if you want to be positive.

Worth noting, this is by no means suggesting that when you are sad or fed up, you don't talk about it. That matters and is important. But dwelling on every niggle without noticing what you have - that is a bad idea.

Back to Toby. He is right, positivity can be tricky, and we have our ancestors, specifically the bears and caves to blame. Your brain is wired to look out for bears coming to steal and eat your food. By default, we are programmed to watch out for attacks, the negative things. Still hundreds of thousands of years later our subconscious by default looks out for danger. We might be attacked, and it wants to protect us. The really good news is that now we sleep with food in a fridge and locks on our doors, safe from the bear attack.

When the negative shows up it can reinforce our previous thoughts and predictions about what could happen, all this energy spent dwelling on the negative. To be positive requires intention. It may mean acknowledging when things go wrong and creating your response. After all, you are not a tree!

If you are to be intentional about being positive, turn off the news! In training, I share the story of Sighing Sandra. Chances are you will recognise her and most likely know someone who is just like her.

Sighing Sandra was known for her frequent sighing throughout the day. The relentless sighing was draining, dull and infectious. Sighing Sandra sighed about everything, really, everything. Waking up with a sigh, getting breakfast with a sigh, the bus a sigh, walking into work with a sigh, sitting down, standing up, make a brew all with a sigh. Sighing Sandra sighed mostly about the world, politics, energy, the economy, the environment, and royalty. She also sighed about the weather, transport, the euro, and sport. Sandra's go-to fuel for sighing was the news. Checking notifications before bed, going to sleep thinking how awful something might be tomorrow, waking up to a notification about how something even more awful could happen and a reminder of the awful thing that still might happen. Then the radio in the shower, Sandra liked the radio in her shower although she did sigh at the price. As the water fell over her, she sighed as the newsreaders shared how the future economic results could be awful. Breakfast with the news offered even more awful, doom, and gloom that may happen one day. The bus stop was an opportunity for Sighing Sandra to share with other commuters the forecast of doom, gloom and dismay that might follow. Headphones and more of the same and into work with a heavy sigh as she felt a duty to share how terrible life in the future could be.

Aah! Sandra began each day weighed down with an overwhelming dollop of negativity. She then looked to share the negative and by default make the big dollop bigger in her head and plant it on others. Aah again. TURN OFF THE NEWS. Be around positive people if you want to be happier and given that happy, positive people sell on average 37% more it's a great starting place.

"All the news, Sally?"
- Ok Toby, tuning in and being informed is a good idea occasionally as long as you are absorbing truth and fact. News that is about what might or may never happen, about what might be said at a speech, presentation, or in a future policy; people shouting at each other and wrapping it up as debate, ill manners, and rude discussion - turn that all off! It is worth noting that sighing Sandra was not best friends with any Presidents and therefore it was unlikely she could influence any of their methods in politics. Her knowledge of transport, energy, the health service, and contacts within it was nil, minimising her ability to influence or change anything. Sandra immersed herself in what she could not control. The sad part is that given 24 hours in any one day, Sandra was wasting hours on what she could not change. Recall the famous Serenity prayer. "Grant me the serenity to accept the things I cannot change, the courage to change the things I can and the wisdom to know the difference." Maybe I could add a bit here. When you work out what you can do or change and find some extra time, use that time wisely. Feed your brain the brilliant stuff, the things that you can build on. Knowledge is at our fingertips daily and for free. Build your knowledge, get passionate about your subject, and become an

authority on what you do. It is of course your call, but remember, you're not a tree.

The crazy part is that if your default setting is negative and you're given positive news, your brain chooses to stay negative. If you're positive and told negative your brain might switch. There have been studies to highlight the benefits of being intentionally positive. It might not be easy all the time, but it can happen if you choose if you are intentional about being positive.

If you are making mistakes, then you are well-placed to learn from them. Every time you hear a "No thank you" when prospecting, you are closer to a "Yes!" If your patter is not on par, there is an opportunity to gain experience, learn and improve. When you look at life with a glass-half-full approach you will smile more and people like being around positive people.

The story of Bee Gee's Bill sees people in training begin to do disco! Like Sandra, you will most likely recognise Bill.

Bill used to be positive, he used to be a top biller at the newspaper. Bill was a mentor to many and respected by most, well, he was back in the day. I had known Bill when he was flying, number 1, the top biller, so visiting the paper and meeting a sad, fed up, pretty scruffy and to be honest, fairly smelly Bill was a shocker. Bill joined me for a walk by the canal, coffee-to-go in hand. Bill looked shattered, needed the coffee to keep himself awake and had become an expert in balancing that and a cigarette in one hand.

"What's up, Bill?" Listening without interrupting and a good hour later, Bill stopped talking. The whole life thing, his wife leaving and left to look after himself was not working out. I asked Bill about his morning routine. He looked at me and said, "What morning routine?" "You know, when you wake up how does your morning look?" "Ok, well, I set the alarm and it bleeps at 7.30 am. I then bash the snooze button for another three minutes, then bash again as the buzzing gets louder. Amazing it still works really! Anyway at 7.45 I know I must move. A quick cigarette in bed first, she would never have allowed that Sally." "I get it Bill. Then what?" "Loo, maybe a shower if time, then a quick smell check and if ok pull on a shirt from yesterday, fly downstairs for coffee, black as there's no milk, another cigarette and then chewing gum as there's no time to brush my teeth and out of the door for 8.55 in the Maestro, which is running on empty and due a service. Usually get to work late but hey, I have been there twenty years, so they are hardly going to fire me."

Clarity landed, smelly, dishevelled, uncaring, this was so sad. "Bill, what do you enjoy doing?"

"Coffee and a cigarette Sally, I enjoy those things and maybe a whisky at the end of the night. But what really makes me smile, it is so silly I smile just thinking about it, is the Bee Gees." I was shocked by the reply but went with it. "The Bee Gee's, Bill? Well, you have surprised me. Which song and why?" "Sally, an all-time favourite legend of a song is Staying Alive and dancing to Staying Alive the whole track for a whole 4 minutes and 10 seconds, have you seen the video, Sally? It's brilliant!" Why this song? Staying Alive seemed ironic given that Bill was living on whisky, coffee, and fags. "Sally, back in the day..." and Bill shared a story about a disco trophy he had won, the outfit, the moves, the attention and adoration he had received.

"Bill, would you do me a small favour?" He said yes before knowing what it would be. I knew he would. "Tomorrow morning and for the next 28 days when you wake up, would you allow yourself an extra 5 minutes in your morning routine to go downstairs or in the garden and put on the Bee Gees track Staying Alive and dance like you did back in the day?" Bill was perplexed and replied, "I figure yes, Sally, why not? Anyway, happy to do you a small favour although I have absolutely no idea why you're asking me to dance each morning, but I trust you so, OK!"

The change was not overnight, but the change did happen. True to his word Bill woke 5 minutes early on day one and danced, smiled, and set off to work a minute earlier in a very slightly different mindset. As the days went on a minute or two earlier, he found time to shower for longer, brush his teeth and by the last week make some porridge by simply adding water. Bill called me after 28 days. "Sally, I plan to keep doing this dance thing, it's pretty cool." Bill's manager called me. "Whatever did you say to Bill? He's changed, in work on time, smiling, calm and heading back to being the A-game Bill we know and love."

The great thing here is that Bill changed everything by changing his morning routine. He committed to five minutes as a favour at first, but he committed. Those five minutes saw him create a new, positive beginning to each day that he built on, a step at a time, or a disco move in Bill's case.

How is your morning routine? Beginning each day with gratitude, and owning your morning routine, sets you up for a winning day. When you find positives, recognise them however small, then build on them and move forward a step at a time, knowing that you achieved something positive yesterday. As you build, remember to say, "Well done" and recognise what you have achieved. Knowledge, experience, a client base - you did it, you began and you're winning. Now that is a positive!

It is easy to brush off achievement, ignore and pass it over, to dismiss it with "Oh, it was nothing." Instead, you could use each win, however small as a building block to a positive future. When you build on activities positive, recognise each success, and understand that you achieved you are setting yourself up for more positive progress.

Extraordinary salespeople are intentional about being positive, they give with a free heart, choose to avoid negative and take action to remain positive.

Time for some clarification. The job title 'salesperson' is loosely hung on shoulders all over the world. The image of a 'salesperson' is cool, slick, and clearly loaded. Imagining the power suit, sharp shoes and immaculate tie and a designer bag as standard. The thing is this label of a 'salesperson' is frequently thrown around casually without any notion of what a real salesperson does.

Often customer service people are promoted into sales roles without training, understanding or, a skill set that could deliver success. Managers approach sales recruitment with a bum on seats and sink-or-swim approach. Get lucky, land a sale, and stay. Most don't and the recruitment plan is to rinse and repeat. It is silly, a waste of money and most importantly massively demoralising to those in sales roles without any training.

Selling is an art, a skill. It requires talent, learning and understanding. It takes time. Time is frequently negated when the bums-on-seat approach is implemented. Sales is a profession.

Simply put salespeople sell. Talented, extraordinary salespeople, hunt, find an opportunity where no one else is looking, ignore recession and understand there is always opportunity. They are driven and gritty. Tenacity is their middle name. It's an attitude thing and guess what, this selling business is hard work, hard work that demands a thick skin, laser focus and a commitment to looking after your health and well-being so that you can consistently be an ultra-high performer.

Hungry salespeople drive their day, invest in themselves and value every minute they have. They see no barriers, blockages or hurdles, they are going all out to win. En route to a call, they listen to an audiobook, podcast, or a book to learn from. They turn off the news and feed their brain the good stuff.

"They feed their brain, Sally?"

- Yes, they feed their brain.
"More brain stuff, I thought we had done that bit?"
- Toby, thank you, a great comment.

The brain is pretty huge and determines daily what you do and how. Top salespeople understand this.
- Toby what did you have for breakfast?
Toby squirms. "A Mars bar, three packets of crisps, a red bull followed by another red bull and some candy floss."
- Really, candy floss?
"Well, only a little as it was left over from the fair".

I often ask this question in training. The responses are mixed, some healthy, some average and sadly, often breakfast is missed. Breakfast is fuel, nourishment and provides energy for you to be sharp and deliver the best version of you. The scientific consensus is simple - eat a nutritious breakfast if you want to be on form and always deliver your A game.

Your brain is also waiting to be fed. You can listen to every news bulletin about world topics that are out of your control, you can read every notification about the news that is truly awful and that you are unable to remedy, you can discuss every news story, and sad tale and dwell in a spiral of uncertainty and negativity about what could, might or may happen one day. Or you can TURN IT OFF

Feed your brain the good stuff. Begin with gratitude. Every day find three things that you are grateful for. This morning one of mine was blackberry and apple crumble, they don't have to be huge, just notice what you are grateful for. The stunning sky, the great meeting, the friendships, water from the tap. When you take note of the small things and you feed your brain good things, (gratitude, learning, success stories), when you note the positives, you create building blocks.
It is all to do with the RAS (Reticular Activating System), the part of your brain that reacts to what you feed it. When you send in

positive, happy thoughts your brain is, well, happy and positive!

Send it worry and doubt and your brain will display worry and doubt. The RAS is unable to distinguish between fact and fake. So put simply - given that this part of the brain is your attitude programmer and you're in control, I would suggest, feeding it fabulous and being, well, fabulous!

3 Achievement!

What is achievement? What does it look like? How do you know when you have it?

Toby looks exasperated. "This is easy Sally! It is target achievement, money in the till, dollar done and target smashed."

Toby is correct - sort of. I have found in sales that achievement is frequently put to one side as another target lands, another deal needs doing or another goal needs to be scored. The phrase, 'You're only as good as your last sale 'is often true.

You go to the races, drink copious amounts of Prosecco and even, on the way home, hang your backside out of the coach whilst singing "Titanium"! Then on Monday, morning you chase around manically because you missed a day celebrating and have so much to do, so busy. You are back on the treadmill.

It is a picture that is evident in sales teams across the UK and having been to many fabulous do's, celebrating growth, successful years, and big wins, for the record with my backside happily seated in the coach) - I agree that they are lots of fun.

The point is though, that not all success, not all wins or achievements require a one-year wait until you celebrate.

Better to celebrate often, to recognise what you have achieved and build on that. Baby steps, a slice at a time, are the only way to 'eat the elephant'. What matters is that you recognise what you are doing, what you are achieving all the time.

Toby has his head back in his hands. He is listening intently. Often in training, I ask the person who has been there the longest how much they know about their job role. Clearly, their knowledge is vast, sometimes twenty years plus. Then I ask how often they congratulate themselves after a day's work for what they have achieved, what they know and their contribution. Usually, this is met with a like, "Really, well, never." So never in twenty-plus years has that person said, "Well done, me"? They now hold twenty years 'worth of knowledge, have twenty years plus of experience and can share twenty years of wisdom. Yet they have never said "Well done!" to themselves? This is often quite thought-provoking for many people.

Next, I might ask the same question to the newest person in the room, someone who has only been there for a few weeks. I ask how it's going and what they have learned since Day 1. The list is often long. "Loads, Sally, loads!" Then I suggest that they know more now about their product or service than they did just a matter of weeks ago. "Yes of course!" The same question follows. "Have you congratulated yourself or said, "Well done!" for what you now know."

Sadly, there is usually another "No!" Oh dear, such a shame that even in the early days, companies omit to deliver the brilliance of "Thank you" and "Well done!" and recognise the achievement of the employee. What makes this very sad is that it costs nothing, zero, nada! Just a minute or two to be in the habit of catching good things happening and flagging them with an encouraging word. The potential return on investment is huge – and employers are missing a trick. The evidence is there about positivity, and companies with a high PQ rating achieve more. This is a quick win.

Toby comments, "My manager rarely raises his eyes let alone says, "Thank you."
-Toby, this is where you not being a tree comes in. We could wait around doing a brilliant job, day in and day out in the hope that the boss might smile or at least utter the words, "Thank you" or "Good job!" Or we can take ownership of the situation so that as a human and not a tree, we set out to achieve today and acknowledge what we have done. That is worthy of a "Well done,

me!" if ever there was one. Waiting for others can be silly, a waste of time and energy. Some do, they sit and wait quietly, listening for those words of encouragement and recognition, yet inside, feeling quietly annoyed that the praise is missing. It can become a spiral of underachievement because they live waiting for the words from someone who might be so busy in their world that they just don't notice. So very sad and an utter waste. You can be an achiever, delivering brilliantly if you stop giving the power of how you feel to someone else. Recognise what **you** achieve each day and then the exciting part - you create foundations to build on.

Think about gardening. You pop an acorn into a pot of soil and put it to one side. You hope that someone else will water it, feed it, put it in the sun and repot it as it grows. You leave the food, nourishment, and attention to chance.

But if you plant the acorn, water it, feed it, put it in the warmth and re-pot when needed, when you recognise growth so feed it again and support it, then suddenly you are creating a new tree. (Not that you are one, of course, we have covered that!).

Don't wait for words from others to enable you to live your day in style. Give yourself the "Well done, me!" Recognise your achievements and build on them.

In sales, a new starter is unlikely to win business with a big fish on Day 1. They might however make a call, receive a mobile number, an email address or get an appointment. Perhaps a LinkedIn connection is confirmed, rapport is built with Ethel, the gatekeeper and information about the event their prospect is attending. Clearly, none of these tiny successes constitutes a sale but they are achievements. When added together, these achievements put the new starter a step closer to meeting the prospect. Some go for sighing and complaining that they have not won a big fish on Day 1. Time for a reality check! You are moving forwards. Say, "Well done, me!" Come to work the next day ready to keep moving forward. All the action points, achievements and tiny successes when backed up with consistency will put you in front of a decision-maker. If, however, after Day 1 you go home cross, gutted, and fed up that you did not close a deal, then your mindset for tomorrow morning is less than positive.

If new to customer experience, training, in the beginning, looks at the basics, being clear, waiting to hang up after the customer, and listening without 'but', all before learning the systems. Then how to be empathetic, build rapport, laugh, and bring positivity to a call. Only when the basics are habitual and just 'what you do' will second sales, anchoring, mop up, cross-sell and upselling be new habits to learn. Learning everything in week one would be overload and daunting. By breaking it down, a module or a bite at a time then practicing creating an unconscious habit achievement begins. Adding to your skill set is made easier when you remember to praise your success along the way.

It is critically important to recognise your success and achievement. Otherwise, negativity, dissatisfaction and unease set in. Remember you are not a tree so it's time to own the fact that you drive your day; you control what you feed your brain and recognising what you have achieved is a great place to start.

Being positive is easier when you recognise each achievement and build on them all.
Remember - positive people sell more.

4 Time

We think it does, that we are in control and that everything can be done in our own time, tomorrow, next week. It is easy to put work to one side, it can wait, later, mañana.

"Sally, what does time have to do with selling?"
- Everything Toby, everything! Salespeople are paid to sell; it is easy to understand that right? Yet so often salespeople put off, put to one side, and avoid the actual selling.

Every day you and I have exactly the same amount of time. A whole 24 hours! Prestigious business leaders often include this fact in presentations and underline the importance of being effective with your day. Still, we ignore, sloth and pretend like we have all the time in the world.

When the lightbulb moment arrives and you realise that time is not standing still, is precious and tomorrow is not a guarantee, then, then you can be effective with time. Remember you're not a tree, you can choose to drive your day, and choose how you use your time and that is super exciting.

It begins with knowing your priority and managing your time, but like all stories, there has to be a beginning and the beginning is **Priority**. What's yours?

- Toby, what is your priority in life? Not just work, day job or, to-do list, what is your priority in life?"
Toby squirms, "I have never really thought about it Sally, it's kind of tricky."

He is right it is. I never thought about it either until 2021. I had vision boards, clear goals, and a plan but no real priority. Like Toby, I found the question uncomfortable, felt as if I was having to rank family, friends, and work. Now, and thanks to 2021 I get it.

February 2021, waking up on a Sunday morning and ouch. Big huge whopping humungous ouch, pain, agony more pain. Without any notable lifting, twisting or, sudden movement my back was in spasm and out of order. Quite simply, and in part a result of the Covid pandemic, I'd been sitting down too long, way too long. Thanks to an amazing osteopath and a few tablets all was well a few weeks after. The weeks when it was out of order I slept on the floor and crawled to the loo like a combat soldier crawling under a net, only in PJs, on carpet and way slower. Eating on the floor, unable to work, go upstairs or, do pretty much anything. Life at 100mph suddenly halted.

It was a brilliant wake-up call and now I am truly grateful. Those moments were an opportunity to weigh up what mattered. Business, however important, was not as important as health. When health goes your ability to do business is gone, and to be a good mum, wife and friend is all sidetracked. Health now sits firmly as my priority.

Toby looks up, "But that is just a given surely?"
 - Maybe for some Toby, but since making it my priority it is at the base of every decision I make, especially tricky ones. Walking regularly, building core strength, and looking after my health now takes priority over everything. The last-minute booking or call with a client, having a clear set priority gives me a benchmark.

It is the same in business, when a business understands and shares what its priority is, then there is a clear benchmark.

Think Ryan Air. Usually, I mention their name to be met with groans and dissatisfaction about the time people flew with them. Ryan Air is unapologetic in its priority to be profitable and make money. They find an opportunity to charge for an extra bag, check-in, sandwich, seat, or drink. You will probably walk across the tarmac to your plane before taking an uncomfortable seat. They don't care about the experience; they care about getting you from A to B and making a profit in the process.

If you're looking for customer experience, turn to Virgin. The smiles, warm welcome, goodie bags and speedy check-in are all a part of your journey. The beautiful lounge, delightful cabin crew even a limo to the airport if you choose. Virgin wants you to leave the flight happy and raving about them so you will want to use them again. Their priority is your happy experience.

Both airlines have clear priorities that are shared both internally and externally with customers. To expect a Virgin experience from a Ryan Air £20 super ticket is silly, misguided and never going to happen. Both businesses will, however, be successful because they know, (and so do their customers), what their priority is.

When you know your priority, in business or life, it makes creating vision, mission and values so much easier. Do they link back to your priority?

"Can you have two priorities Sally?" asks Toby.

When companies try to bring in two priorities, Toby, confusion is created. A story for you!

There was a supermarket chain, A Very Big Super Market. The board, struggling to decide on the priority, choose to go with two. To delight customers and to keep the shelves full at all costs. The board visited all stores to share the two priorities over a buffet lunch and presentation. They backed the visits up with a letter to all employees as well as leaving fancy posters for the staff room, corridors, and warehouse. The priorities were known and understood, after all, they had been delivered by the board in person!

Stacey had worked at The Very Big Supermarket for over 5 years, the job fitted around her children. Her aisles were fresh bakes and cakes. Stacey was always proud of how they looked and together with her team kept the shelves full and appealing. It was tricky for some days, especially when people were off or when they were super busy.

One day, Morris visited the Very Big Super Market for cake. Morris, 74, was partial to cake and as it was his wife's birthday a big cake was in order, but which one? Morris rarely went to the supermarket by himself, especially not for cake. Morris asked for help. The lady was busy refilling shelves. Stacey was stuck, did she stop and help Morris with his cake choice, show him the options and offer a sample or stay stacking the depleted isles? This morning it looked like they had been raided. Stacey, a great employee, was genuinely stuck between a rock and a hard place, or in this instance a cake aisle and Morris. What to do?

Toby nodded in agreement, "I see Sally, two is too confusing."
- Yes, Toby! Priorities can change, they often do, but knowing yours in business and life is a great way to make every minute of your 24 hours fall in line with what you're looking to achieve. It is just the beginning though.

5 People Buy You

When you set out in business you are often in a hurry to sell to everyone. Of course, every single person on the planet will love what you do - after all, you do!

Your product and service are unsurpassable and your enthusiasm for this sensational, new innovation is unstoppable, as it should be when you begin.

So, you set off on Day 1 and the website goes live! You sit waiting for enquires and orders to flood in, for your phone to ring and notifications of transactions to be on loop.

But nothing! All is quiet, silent in fact. No calls, no emails, and no notifications. What is going on? Your website took months, your logo is a thing of beauty and your social media posts are simply stunning. Still silence.

You check your Wi-Fi, broadband and even unplug the computer to blow on the cable, turn it on and off again in true IT support style - but still nothing.

It is the same in a sales role. On Day 1 of your new job, you're excited, enthusiastic, and loving the product, service and, company. The values are right up your street, you buy into the mission and agree with their ways of working. You sit and wait for sales, but nothing comes. You check your login, that your mobile works and that your tech is set up correctly. Just in case, you unplug, blow on the cable, switch on and off again, but still nothing. IT smile knowingly, they have seen this many times before.

The reason for this nil response is simple. However great your SEO, PR, or website, *you are not known*. Your logo is fab, your website slick and your product superb, but your future customers don't know you.

Toby looks puzzled. "A good website matters though?" Yes, a fab website is a good idea, but it is not what people buy. Customers and prospects might like your logo or social media posts, but they don't buy them either. They buy *you*!

People buy you when they like and trust you. It's a brain thing! A limbic brain thing to be precise. Understanding this, combined with "Big fish go slow" is a realistic starting point when selling.

The most referred-to slide in my training talks about Lucy, Lovely Lucy. It shows a picture of her in a fabulous coffee shop that she runs in Knaresborough, North Yorkshire. Lucy says her coffee and cakes are excellent and delicious and everyone would enjoy them. Toby pipes up, "Of course she does, it's her coffee shop!" Exactly, Toby, you are correct. The next slide shows a picture of Tom with Lucy, enjoying coffee and cake in her coffee shop. Tom says, "The coffee and cake, in particular the apple and cinnamon cake, are delicious. I always go there when looking for a warm and friendly welcome."

"So, Tom likes Lucy's place then - but what has this to do with the brain?" questions Toby.

Your brain and Tom's are made up of different sections. This can be pictured as a circle with an inner circle. The outer circle is your Neocortex - big and clever. The neocortex loves data, a chart, graphs, or numbers. It can digest a figure, price or quote and mull over designs for days. Visit a technology or electrical store and as the enthused assistant lists the data, spec, ram and speed, your neocortex goes wild! However, your neocortex is also flawed. Massively flawed. Simply, it cannot, will not and never has made a decision. That responsibility goes to the limbic brain.

This is like a different section or department, shown as the inner circle. The limbic brain is smaller and yet powerful. It says, "Yes" or "No". That is all! It buys or doesn't buy, agrees, or doesn't agree. The basis of this is all-powerful, based on emotion. "How do I feel about you? Do I like you; do I trust you?" This is such a massive function and critically important, that it is worth repeating.

Your potential client's limbic brain decides whether to do business with you based on emotions and feelings. "Do I like you and do I trust you?" Understand that and everything else will follow!

Toby shuffles, "But what about price, it always comes down to price?"

Price and how to position yourself in your marketplace is a module on its own, but price is not the sole reason people buy. Studies have found that 33% of people buy on price and it's worth noting that if they do buy on price, they usually walk for the same reason. Time after time people buy because they like and trust you. It is why Tom always goes back to Lucy's coffee shop and why he only ever recommends Lucy's. Can you recall times when you liked the shop assistants so you bought the extra whatever it is? Or do you trust the process so use, say, Amazon although it may be more expensive than going direct? Like and trust drives our day. It is the emotion part again - how do people feel about you?

When your customers love what you do, and trust that they are valued, then they become your sales force, part of your prospecting mix. Their opinion about you and how you help them do business is way more trusted by others than anything you could say about yourself. We trust strangers 'opinions over an individual's.

In training, I will ask a question. - How are you delighting, looking after, and building relationships with your existing customers? Are they referring you just because? Just imagine how, if they did, the growth could look.

Toby is smiling, "Ok, so that kind of makes sense and is also mind-blowing. But you mentioned something about fish going slow?"

"Big fish go slow". I created this phrase as a reality check. Often when people go on a sales workshop, a day course, read a sales book or do an online module, they learn a sales process.

Using a process is a great idea and in future chapters, you will learn an 11-step process proven to deliver sales and results.

However, soon after completing such training, most people claim it doesn't work. They have read the book once, spent an hour online and maybe even done role-play in a fancy hotel. Like driving or baking all new processes require practice and the reason it might not have worked is usually down to timing and lack of practice.

Imagine, Trainee Trev meets a new prospect for the first time. They looked ideal and matched his target profile. Trev goes wild, pulls out his sales card and begins the steps. Starting at step 1 and heading right through to 11, he takes notes, which was suggested as a good idea. Within a minute or maybe two he builds rapport and when pitching, he is textbook through and through.

Trev takes under 50 minutes to complete the sales process for a prospect who is a stranger. The prospect says, "No!" Trainee Trev is perplexed, totally baffled. It never went like this in the role-play.

This result, however, was predictable. The prospect's limbic brain does not know, like or trust Trev, yet. He might be a nice guy; have a fabulous product and he could probably help. Right now though, in less than an hour, however slick the process there is no like or trust.

Trev is annoyed, he spent weeks in training and clearly, that was a waste of time. They promised that if you followed the process it would work.

A reality check! People, you, and me, like to take time to get to know other people, especially when looking to work with them and invest in what they offer. This requires a relationship and relationships take time to build.

The bigger the commitment required and the investment to be made, the slower the fish goes. Big fish go slow. Sometimes it can take years to cement a deal, land an opportunity or nail the sale. Impatience, believing that if you follow the steps in one go and boom wow you're sorted, is but a myth. You have been sold!

When you understand that big business opportunities are often created when you know, like and trust each other, and that takes time, you are winning.

Park the process until you need it. Begin work on getting to know your prospect, and ensure they like and trust you. This takes time, commitment, patience and maybe just a coffee. Truly successful people recognise this.

6 It's Just a Coffee!

That is all it is - a coffee. Park the agenda, the hidden intention and have a coffee.

Time for context and the importance of follow-up. Follow-up could be a whole chapter but for now, back to coffee.

Trainee Trev was brand new to his business development role and at the suggestion of booking a follow-up coffee, he looked very doubtful. "A coffee, Sally?"
- Yes, a coffee.
"But won't they ask loads of questions, want information and detail about what we sell? Because I know very little."

Trev's knowledge of the industry was just three weeks 'worth. But by the time coffee came around, he would have gained more industry experience and knowledge. Trev's hesitation came from a lack of understanding that coffee is just that, a coffee. It is definitely not a sale, a pitch or a presentation, it is just the beginning of getting to know someone. Remember, big fish go slow.
For Trainee Trev, a lack of confidence also played a part, understandable given that he was new to both the sector and the role.

You will most likely never know every single detail about your company, what it offers or the services it provides. This is especially true when, like Trainee Trev you are only three weeks into a new role.

Recruiters rarely know every tiny detail about the sectors for which they are recruiting. They will have a good understanding and continue to learn as the years tick by. There is no need to know every detail about everything when having "Just A Coffee."

A coffee is just that, a coffee. It provides an opportunity to meet a new contact, or an existing one and chat, learn about each other, what you both do and how or if you can help them.

Toby raised his head, "You have lost me, Sally, I'm with the new chap, Trev! Surely you need something?"

- Toby, let's imagine for a minute, unexpectedly you meet the love of your life on a night out. You are dazzled, see the long-term commitment and a wonderful future relationship. You feel a buzz at the thought of getting married, having children, and retiring together. The only slight flaw in this idealistic dream of yours is that the person you met a minute or two ago and have fallen for has absolutely no clue what you are thinking and is quite happy enjoying a drink with you and getting to know you.

Let's take it a step further. You decide that, as you are so committed and passionate about your future together then they need to know, must know, surely, they feel what you feel. As they politely sip a drink, just moments since meeting you, the words fall from your mouth. "Shall we get married, have children and grow old together, sail into the sunset in later years?" If on audible, please add a big screech to a sudden halt! The person you have asked to marry you holds their drink still and stares at you in disbelief. She goes to open her mouth in horror but instead of replying, she grabs her bag, puts down the drink and runs. She runs so fast that you are left with two drinks and your hopes of any future with this wonderful, perfect person dashed. You drink both drinks, quickly. Later when you try calling, you're blocked, your emails hit firewalls and on arrival at their office security won't even let you past the barriers. You have officially crashed and burned!

It's not a pretty story, it screams of desperation and someone needy, very needy. For those who have read Dr Cialdini's Principals of Influence, the Romeo and Juliet effect of scarcity and wanting what is just out of reach was all forgotten. The results; a disastrous date and certainly no further relationship.

Back to big fish going slow! So far, we have talked about building relationships, the importance of trust, like and understanding the limbic brain - but how? This is where coffee comes in. You cannot get to know someone by firing off emails. You cannot build a trusting relationship where you know and understand the problems in their business by sending out multiple brochures, flyers, or invitations. The whole thing about being human is that we want to meet, talk, engage. There is power in a face-to-face meeting, sitting, sharing, learning, and importantly reading all the other intricacies to understand what is not being said verbally. Your phone call will stand out as your competitors send multiple email threads in the hope that one might peak, attract interest, and generate a click-through. Their success is doubtful compared to your own. The special offer, one day only and super discount are long forgotten once you have met, got to know, and nurtured a relationship with your client or prospect.

Time. This is a biggie! It takes time, maybe a coffee, tea, lunch, dinner, golf, or even maybe axe throwing! Meeting at an exhibition, then coffee or lunch, and taking time with a prospect or client is a good idea.

When, if you're married or in a long-term relationship, did you decide to take it to the next step, move in, adopt a puppy, or get married? Was it when it **felt** right? Rarely does this happen on a first date. We value time, learning about each other, habits, likes, and dislikes. This is when the magic happens when trust and liking are built. Given that the limbic brain oversees decision-making and is driving your future sale, then trust and liking matter.

Toby is nodding, he looks up and asks, "How do you suggest a coffee? Is that not a bit, well, odd?"
- Signposting plays a part here, Toby. When you meet the person, realise that they would be good in your network and look like an

ideal prospect, suggesting in conversation that you might meet in the future for coffee, to learn about what they do, is easy. It's just chatting, banter, just what you do - after all this is business. Then post the event, preferably a call that they will be expecting or a LinkedIn message, suggesting a coffee. Again, signposted as an hour just to get to know them. Some will decline and some will accept, either way, you begin to build your network. Importantly, approach prospects in a non-salesperson, double glazing, timeshare, pushy Wolf of Wall Street way. That will only send people running for the hills and blocking your calls.

The important part of this is that you begin. It might seem scary especially if your communication methods are mostly tech-based. To build confidence, for it to be less scary you simply must do it. You must make the call and then show up. Each time you do it, the process becomes easier.

Now for a top tip that was mentioned to me by an aspiring gentleman Richard Field OBE, the car park email.

After you have met, somewhere quiet and conducive to good conversation. After you have enjoyed their company and learned a little more, suggest meeting again, staying in touch and maybe catching up at a future event. When you are back in the car, pull out your phone and ping an email, short and sweet.

"Mr Prospect, good to meet you for coffee, an enjoyable hour learning about you, thank you."

Any detailed follow-ups can come later. Remember to record your notes for the future and that's it! If you're thinking that this is a bit over the top, well, in a world where being liked and trusted enables decisions to be made then being on your client's or prospect's radar, building familiarity and awareness in a positive, polite way, is a great idea. Try it! It works by making people smile and **feel** good and enjoy "Just A Coffee".

7 A Fabulous First Impression!

Dynamic Doug was a successful business leader with the ability to truly understand people ahead of placing them into interim roles within huge organisations. The context, say a large high street retailer wanted to implement change A new process, system or even culture can be tricky if your existing team has closed minds or are not enthused about the proposed change. To drive change would need a strong, personable leader who in a matter of months could implement change with minimal fallout and disruption. Doug paid sizeable salaries to the right people to do this but unfortunately, the right person was not always easy to find.

The role would be advertised and the applicants, many. CV's read like a dream, A levels, lots of stars, degrees, many first class and a few masters thrown in. Certificates, achievements and even trophies are listed, noted, and often <u>underlined</u> and **bolded** to emphasise just how good they were. Their intelligence was undisputed, however, what Doug needed did not come with a certificate or trophy. Doug was looking for emotional warmth, the ability to build and nurture relationships, an understanding that everything is people-based and an ability to read body language, voice tone and even a glance. Doug wanted way more than many thought. It was his attention to what was not on the CV that saw change happen across the UK as he placed extraordinary people into challenging roles.

His success resulted in rather fabulous offices across the UK, with his flagship being in London, next door to St Paul's Cathedral and not far from the First Dates restaurant. It was bling in a non-tacky way reflecting warmth, style, and quality. It oozed professional and yet felt homely. Creating the feel had cost plenty and Doug felt it was worth every thousand pounds invested. He wanted people to feel a certain way on arrival and paying for a design that enabled that was a gift. Doug understood the customer experience was his script to write.

The reception area was stunning and Brenda, who staffed the desk, was a total delight. Brilliant Brenda was early 60's, a grandma and loved her job. She was proud of her reception area and with a small team, they ensured everything worked beautifully. Deliveries were accepted with a smile, passers-by popping in were greeted warmly and applicants for a new role received a sincere smile, the offer of a sit-down and a brew. Brenda made people feel welcome, at home and comfortable.

The applicants were the most fun, thought Brenda. On occasion they would smile, thank her for the drink and begin a cheerful conversation. Enquiring about the design, this week's flowers, or London as a whole. They would chat for a while and thank Brenda a second time, maybe enquire where the toilets were. Brenda would show them and reassure them that there was plenty of time. In a matter of minutes, the beginnings of a friendship were created. That is how Brenda was viewed by most of Doug's team. To the people he had placed over the years and to his business partners, Brenda was their friend and it all started in reception in a matter of minutes.

Then there were the others, those who somehow slipped through the net. The suited young man walked in with a power pose and demanded to see Doug as he had an interview. He refused to sit and stayed hand on his hips looking like he was supercharged and on a mission. The candidate who arrived late blamed everything and everyone but herself and told Brenda that Doug would see her after all she was related to someone very, very important. The candidate who shuffled in so quietly sat down and refused eye contact, conversation or a brew, Brenda was puzzled! The newly graduated young man who brought his Mum in case he got lost. The lady who pleaded and begged, she needed this job and heard Doug was a good payer! Many had little understanding of the importance of a great first impression. They might put on a smile, deliver a firm handshake when entering the top floor boardroom, they might share excellent stories of success, CVs with stars and a list of who they knew that also knew Doug, but it was all wasted. The interview began in the reception with Brenda.

Doug was of course courteous and at the end of the interview would see them to the lift door, sometimes very quickly. His next call, allowing a few minutes for them to leave, would be to Brenda. What first impression had they made with her and her team? That was the most important part. If he received a fabulous response then you were en route to a second interview but if not, you were yesterday's news.

Seven seconds! Try counting seven seconds. That is all it takes to create a first impression. Even less on Zoom - that takes about three. How important then, given that we remember first impressions way longer than what follows, to make sure the first impression you create is a fabulous one.

Let's start with a **smile**, a superpower that we all have. A smile can be delivered with warmth and ease, no words are needed. Make it the first thing you do on arrival, anywhere with anyone. Share a big, wonderful authentic smile.
Seeing that smile the other person's brain is reading you and deciding. You are smiling at me, therefore; you must be nice and so I like you. All this going on in a matter of mere seconds! Remember that 'like 'comes from the limbic part of the brain, the part that makes decisions. Pretty handy that, so start as you mean to go on!

Smile, really smile, not a funny face or dodgy look up then straight back down sort of smile. A Duchenne smile is where the face smiles and regardless of age, your crow's feet are displayed. It's a thing, really it is, try it!

Be **prepared**. This is also covered in Step 1 of the sales process. If you are prepared you are most likely going to arrive in good time, with a swash of confidence, ready to begin the meeting or work the room at an event, whatever it might be.

How do you **look**? This topic can ignite debate! "It should not matter how I look; I should be judged on what I say, on fact, not what I wear or how I look."

You are correct and you should be judged on fact, what you say, the goods you sell and the service you deliver. How you look should make not one jot of difference. But it does because you are meeting other people, human beings with brains and they will, in a matter of seconds, make a judgement based on what they see, before even beginning or getting close to a conversation. Is this fair? Maybe not but life is not perfect or fair. It is simply how it is.

Have you read Dr Cialdini's Six Principals of Influence? He brilliantly shares Principal Six, "Authority." It backs up the importance of dressing to impress, if you want to impress and sell more that is. Simply, your brain shortcuts to 'they must be smart, clever, in charge, trusted', based on what a person wears. We obey a policeman because he wears a uniform, an agent because he flashes a badge, and a judge because she wears a wig. There is a good reason con artists will go to great lengths to make sure their dress suggests we should trust them.

If you want to sell more and have happier customers, show up looking the part, reflect your company beautifully and be trusted and liked. Additionally, if you dress to impress you will walk taller, and feel more confident and this radiates. If you fall short of the fabulous first impression of delivering the goods or service, you will in future lose the business. If your first impression is lacking, then the likelihood of you ever getting even a whiff of a business opportunity is much reduced.

Toby has his thinking face on. "Is it like lucky pants?"
- Yes Toby, it is exactly that. Back in the day when going to Mr. Craig's Nightclub, kicking out time was exactly 2 am and the

kebab shop was a must. Before you went out, or "out-out" as it's now known you would get ready. The time spent preparing to go out, hair, shoes, outfit, fragrance, was immense. You would arrive home smelling like a packet of cigarettes with a whiff of kebab sauce, but it did not matter. You invested time and thought into how you would look and most importantly, feel when you entered that nightclub, walked down the stairs, and headed to the bar to buy a bottle of Hooch! It was of its time and perfectly demonstrates how, if we put effort into how we look, we feel better and walk taller! Men talk of wearing lucky pants, pulling pants and point-blank refuse to wear any other pants. Maybe this is just Toby's story, but I am sure you are getting the point.

A final thought is often shared in training. Imagine you did something really silly on Saturday night, so silly you vaguely recall what it was but are quite sure that it was not you that did that silly thing and if it was you then it needs to go away as it could affect your, up until now, promising promotion! You are due to attend Leeds Magistrates Court on Monday morning. Since sobering up you put in a call and requested a solicitor, just in case. You arrive on time in a suit, tie, and polished shoes. Your solicitor is due to meet you at 9.40 am. There is no sign of anyone. There is however a young man looking down at his scruffy trainers, waiting by the security entrance. He has a duffel bag on his shoulders and is wearing grey joggers with a label, his hoody matches. Maybe he is en route to the gym or has just been for a run. Time passes, it is now 9.45 am and you need to be in Court 2 shortly. No sign of your solicitor. A few minutes later and the man in joggers walks towards you. He is unshaven and you can smell him from here, he must have been running, you think. Much to your surprise he greets you, "Are you Mr. Smith!" Reality dawns and lightbulbs flash in your head. This is your solicitor, whom you paid thousands for! Now you are scared and doubting. Your chances of getting acquitted of doing that really silly thing that you might or might not have done, are on the floor!

In seconds, like it or not, our brains quickly make impressions of the people around us. You can use this knowledge and have it work for you. If you do, you will sell more and have happier customers.

Look appropriate for where you are going, be clean, smart and reflect your company. If you're looking to do business with this person or showcase your company knowing the average value order is £500k then rocking up in joggers and a hoodie covered in dog hair and smelling of yesterday's fry-up is not going to make a great impression.

Toby looks up "How about the tie, Sally?"
- Another brilliant question Toby, thank you.

Once when training in London I was surprised by how few men in suits were wearing ties. I posted on LinkedIn and the debate was big! Toby, it's your call. If you're going all out to reflect your business and you feel a tie is appropriate, wear a tie. If the people you are meeting wear ties, wear a tie. Common sense needs to kick in. My grandfather always looked smart, invariably wearing a shirt and tie with a pullover even in his last days. That impression lasted a lifetime.

Listening and **punctuality** go hand in hand when talking about creating a fabulous first impression. Being on time is an absolute must, better still be early. Sit in reception, chat with Brenda, absorb the company feel and culture, re-check your notes, and be ready for your meeting. Being late delivers a huge insult, suggests that the prospect's time is of little importance and that you're not all that fussed about doing business with them. No amount of traffic, weather, kids, car, or dog will do it, they are lame excuses. Be On Time!

Toby is standing up now. "Sally, that's a bit harsh, isn't it?"
- Toby there will be occasions when an unexpected thing

happens that prevents us from being on time. Maybe annually, maybe even less frequently than that. The important thing to know is that being on time makes customers and prospects happy, they like you, limbic brain. Being late does the opposite, it is ill-mannered. The most incredible lesson worth noting is that today we have traffic and weather, yesterday there was traffic and weather and guess what? Tomorrow there will be traffic and weather. In the same way, as seasons come and go, traffic and weather will be there, and you can choose to work with them and factor in extra time or you can choose to be late!

Give people your time if you're early and they offer then begin early. When people talk, give them time to share. When you ask a question allow them time to reply. The more time your prospect or client has, the more time they talk. The more they talk, the greater the likelihood that they will share what they are looking to buy. Given that your customer's or prospect's most important person is themselves, give them plenty of time to talk about their most important person.

Be careful because if you're not listening this opportunity could be wasted. The chapter on Say Less, Sell More stresses the importance of listening. When looking to make a fabulous first impression, listening as the prospect or customer talks is key. You listening as they talk, equals them liking you. Clever how the brain works!

When having a coffee, at a sales meeting, or attending an event, remember you have one shot at making a first impression, so make it a good one.

8 Say Less Sell More

The module has only just begun, and Toby's hand is already up. "Really, Sally? Surely selling is all about the chat, the banter, slick presentation, and delivery, and that is before knowing your product, company history and terms inside out and sharing them?"

Toby speaks for many a salesperson who thinks that to sell, you need to be chatty, engaging, full of life and easily able to light up a room. This module is not about presentation skills. Mostly it is about being able to listen, really listen, the absolute opposite of what many people in business do. Often, in such a rush to push their special offer, one-day-only deal, they talk at you and rarely, well, shut up.

In training, I ask the team to stand up. It helps, really helps if they remember the Asda adverts from the 1990s when everything was Asda price and the person pushing the trolley would turn back to the camera before gently smacking their bottom to reinforce how much money they had saved. This exercise is the same. I say, "Listen - without butt!" and the team on cue gently smacks their own butt. It takes a few goes, reinforces the "listen without but" message and, is usually met with and ends with laughter, a whole lot of fun.

What on earth does 'listening without but 'even mean?The thinking kicks in, and the replies along the lines of "Listen, Sally, like really listen?"
They are correct, sort of. To really listen, actively listen, you need to 'listen without but'.

Usually, when you are listening to someone, such as a colleague, because you are a polite person you might nod and look engaged but secretly under that nod and eye contact you are creating your next comment, reply, a statement that just has to be shared because clearly, it matters way more than the person speaking. As you're proudly putting your next few, rather fabulous words together your brain is not listening to what is being said. What is being said had moved on and you didn't even realise. Next, you interrupt with a big BUTT and off you go with the control of the conversation back in your hands. Now you're happy and feel as though you are being well listened to. Chances are you're not and the other person is now, in their brain, creating a next point of view, reply or, statement that they are excited to put across. So, wait for it, here comes another BUTT! It is like sparring in a ring, tit for tat or table tennis. It's a competition and yet the power, the real power in conversation, especially with sales, is listening. Listening without butt!

Wing It Wayne whom you will get to know further in future chapters was brilliant at talking to and at people, often referred to as the "Show Up and Throw Up." His ability to listen was terrible and his sales or lack of reflected his lack of listening skill. Listening is an art, that takes time to master and perfect.

Toby raises his hand. "Sally, "it's just listening, open your ears and you're off."
 - If it was that easy, Toby, people would sell a lot more.

Ahead of moving further into this module, it's time to mention Julian Treasure, a master of his craft and that craft is sound, noise and listening. He has written many a fabulous book, talked on TED and been interviewed for high-profile podcasts, most recently Steven Bartlett Diary of a CEO. I recommend you seek him out. Taking time to read or listen and immersing yourself in this magnificent subject, can only help you improve your listening skills and the ability to create and nurture quality relationships in business.

Back to Toby. If only listening was that easy!
- Toby, shall we go outside?
The team comes too, of course. Fortunately, it is a warm

autumnal day and there's plenty of green space. The exercise is to stand a fair distance apart and in the next three minutes remain in silence, not a word, fidget or foot scuff, just absolute silence. In your silence, your task is to note the sounds that you hear.

I love the impact of this task! People stand there, sometimes awkwardly and start to fidget. Odd, but three minutes is tricky for some people. They look to make eye contact or shuffle - anything but be silent. This is not surprising in a world where we surround ourselves with noise - the radio first, the bleep alarm on our phone, YouTube, Alexa, the TV, the kids, cars, and more chatter and noise. It is just that - noise. When the three minutes are over, the sounds people hear are many, birds singing, wind blowing, generators humming, cars whizzing, people talking, doors slamming, crates banging, and aircraft flying. Many sounds are identified in only three minutes.

The next question seems to be a hard one.
- Tell me, when was the last time you were standing still, in silence, for three minutes? Often this elicits a laugh as though to say, "Do you think I have three minutes to be still and silent?"

Three minutes in 24 hours to be still and silent, not a full-scale meditation. Three minutes is a whole 0.2% of your day! If you're in business, then being a better listener is a skill that will see you sell more. Investing in your skill set is an excellent idea and as you're not a tree, choosing to take three minutes a day is a good place to start. Back to the task.

The team is still standing and is back to chatting. Next as a generous gift, I hand over a fictitious £250 ticket to Wembley. We are all going to see a famous, iconic musician. I ask them to choose who, the replies vary from Adele and Beyoncé to Cliff Richard. Sir Cliff Richard is an excellent choice but embracing my inner Beyoncé is much easier. Pretending, mic in hand, I begin to sing with gusto, embracing my inner Beyoncé!

I tell the team that they are really enjoying the singing, the atmosphere and everything about the concert. Then I ask,
- Are you listening to me, Beyoncé, or are you hearing me?
They go quiet, suddenly unsure if this thing that they have been doing with their ears since birth is listening or hearing, often unaware there is even a difference.

Doubtful replies, hearing, listening, a bit of both?

I flip the question and ask if Beyoncé would be listening to or hearing her crowd as they sing along, dance and cheer. Now the doubtful looks grace most faces. Toby is perplexed and asks, "There is a difference?"

Yes, there definitely is a difference. Hearing is where we spend most of our time. Hearing is background noise, coffee shops, the supermarket, and the radio. It is noise that is just there, and we are not tuned into it unless our name is called. Background noise and hearing are where we spend most of our time. Hearing is what Beyoncé does - she hears a mass of noise. OK, the crowd may call it singing but for Beyonce, she is hearing the noise.

Listening is what you are doing when Beyoncé sings. Hanging onto every word, lyric and inflection. With the musicality, detail, and passion, you're listening to it all.

Rarely do we truly listen. When did you last listen to a bird singing, the wind blow or leaves rustling? In life, we are usually in such a rush that we rarely listen. When you make time to be a better listener, it will help you in business. A task to enhance listening: en route to work, a client meeting or a call, if driving turn off the radio. Be quiet! What sounds do you hear?

The part of being silent, without noise, that is fabulous and worthy of mention - when you are quiet, still and at the moment the most incredible ideas pop into your head space. Cool, fabulous ideas that were previously drowned out by noise can get through. Take this morning's walk, early and quiet, the title for this module. Say, Less, Sell More! Just popped in!

9 It's How You Say It!

If ever there was a subject critically important to how your customers and prospects relate to you, this is it. Not just what you say, the words that come out, but how you say it. Language, words and their impact overlap with customer experience, prospecting, and sales. Deals can be lost on a word, customers infuriated by a phrase and prospects turned off by a comment.

Back to the brain, so much is about the brain and words are no exception. There are many fabulous books written about the brain, in #sallyfact language there is a system one brain that wears trainers and system two brain that does yoga. In training, I ask people to draw the parts of the brain, one wearing trainers and one doing a yoga pose. As we all have a system one and two brain, being able to understand how they react is important.

With its trainers on, the system one brain is fast, automatic. It just does, gives little thought and cracks on. It is a default setting that responds at speed (hence the trainers).

System two brain is meditating, giving it thought and taking time to study the detail. Do you see why yoga is a good fit? System two brain is great at studying, focusing, and understanding the detail, it has a very conscious approach to a topic. The opposite of system one brain.

"Sally, really the brain again, it's just words, language and why am I drawing pictures of a brain doing yoga and wearing trainers?"
- Toby, drawing pictures helps lock the info into your long-term memory, the hippocampus. Storing this long term is a good idea because this next bit is important - easy to do when you know how and so very easy to mess up when you don't.
- You need to understand that your brain, both system one and system two, will react to the words people say to you. Even

more powerful is understanding that when you say certain words to a person, customer, or prospect it can trigger their system one brain positively or more often negatively.
- Toby, it is like being given the most wonderful gift to help you influence your customers and prospects to say yes, be happy and refer.

All the sales processes, customer experience plans and ways to sell more are worthless if the language you use, the words and the way you say them, are flawed.

Toby draws two beautiful-looking brains, system one is not only wearing trainers but running a marathon.

Lets us stay at first with system one brain.

Imagine you see a toddler asking for chocolate, moments before his tea. Mum and Dad loudly say, "No, absolutely not it is nearly tea time, it will ruin your appetite." What does the toddler do? On hearing the word **no** the toddler stomps their feet, crosses their arms, pulls a face and screams. "I want chocolate." More **no no no** from Mum and Dad and they hurry on with tea. The toddler is really unhappy and goes all-out full-on rolling on the floor. The toddler has not heard reason or logic and the word appetite is lost on them, all they heard was NO and, system one brain kicked off. It's how it is wired.

Tea goes on the table, and eventually, the toddler sits up, hanging on to the simple fact they were not able to have chocolate when they wanted. Sulking, the toddler plays with tea, Mum mentions that there is chocolate for pudding but any sense of pretty much anything is not working in the toddler right now. They play with their food, throw bits on the floor, and annoy Mum and Dad.

Tea is swiftly over; chocolate is forgotten about and the toddler now sitting on the naughty step. Over two hours of unpleasantness, all because of one word, no. Fed up toddler, exasperated Mum, and Dad.

Two hours! Two hours could easily have been salvaged if different words had been used.

The sequel uses alternative words.

Imagine you see a toddler asking for chocolate moments before his tea. Mum and Dad say shall we get it ready for pudding after tea. Lovely idea, you made a great pudding choice.

What does the toddler do? Smiles happy that his request has been met with agreement. He and his family will get chocolate for pudding. Mealtime is easy, pudding delicious, happy toddler and happy Mum and Dad.

Have I oversimplified, maybe a little? Toby thinks so,
"Yeh yeh Sally but that is a toddler, and we are adults."
- Good point Toby, that is true, but even adults have a system 1 brain and when it hears the word No, it immediately, without thought, goes into defence mode, ready to take on the world and fight to turn it around, to disagree or sometimes run away.

The system one brain interprets words without thought, **No** is the most annoying of them all. Other words that are accusatory, judgmental and turn people right off are, You **must** do that task, You **should** have completed and I **want** you …

Are you cringing? I did when learning about language. Recalling the times when telling my teenagers they must do, should do because I wanted. Hindsight being a marvelous thing, all these phrases could have been changed and received a far more fruitful response.

Back to business. It is the same. Your choice of words can turn your customers off or, if replaced with alternatives, see them happy, even when delivering bad news. (More of which in a future chapter)

To create an opportunity with a prospect, try language such as 'you might like', 'you could try 'or, 'I would like'. These phrases are much softer than must, should and want. They are the fluffy slippers of language. They mean the same but in the customer's system one brain remains calm and able to make a favorable decision.

One of the most powerful changes in language is replacing **no** or **can't** with **unable**.

An example. Mr Jones, placing his order at 4 pm, wants his grass seed tomorrow morning by 8 am. The courier has left for the day, and you are certain there is no way you can make that happen. Saying an immediate **no** or **can't** guarantees a fed-up and annoyed customer. Maybe try this - I understand why you'd want your grass seed so early, leave it with me and I will see what the other drivers can do. This is step 1 - suggest you are trying to make it work, looking for a solution. Step 2, Mr Jones, I have tried everything and am simply unable to get it to you by 8 am. There is a courier who could have it to you by midday so your planting can go ahead?
At all costs avoid **can't** or **no** and replace with **unable**.

By prefixing with the phrase 'leave it with me 'you are showing that you are trying to find a solution. You could also try 'let me see what I can do'. Anything but a flat-out **no**.

Think back to a time when you made a suggestion only to be met with a no. Recently sharing about an event with a good friend, I thought it might be of use to her and her business. The response, was a flat no! We are still friends but, in that split, second, I thought how rude, and ill-mannered to rule something out before even a thought. It happens unconsciously, your system 1 brain hears 'no 'and thinks 'rude 'or worse!

An exercise to do before learning other words to replace, excite and influence is to become aware of when you say no! Make a note, a tally, you might be surprised.

In training, I share the story of Norman No who as you can guess said no to everything immediately and his polar opposite, Sam the Yes Man. The story is below, enjoy!

Norman No and Sam The Yes Man

"No, just no! That's all that is to be said on the matter. No! No! No!"

"Wow!", thought Sam."Such a heated response to the offer of a cup of tea." Not that Sam was able to actually offer the tea since his knock on Norman's office door was met with the tirade of "No! No! No! and No!"

"Most strange," thought Sam! He was new to the firm, Proctor & Porridge, but he'd heard about Norman and his No's!

Norman's default setting was No! Can't, Won't and if in any doubt, No! Norman was a busy man; his job was full time and every minute was packed with the world's biggest to-do list. He had to crack on. Engaging in conversation with people, whether colleagues or suppliers met with a big "No, too busy". The No's flowed, on email, text, a call, just No!

Over five years in post Norman found that No was an efficient way to deal with most of his days at the firm. Norman used to say Yes, years ago but it led to all sorts of trouble and certainly added to his workload so for now, No suited.

Norman was miserable, unsure how he'd become miserable, but he was. On the rare occasion he ventured to the canteen, he was sure people turned their backs and walked away from him and no one ever joined him for lunch. The last Christmas do was unbearable. Norman had made an effort with a new suit and fragrance and was looking pretty sharp, so he thought. But at the do, no one spoke to or engaged with him. They were all chatting away, laughing in groups, dancing the conga. Norman really wanted to do the conga. He particularly wanted to conga with Debs, but, well no! Instead, he drank whisky doubles with a chaser, it was a free bar after all.

It had been a sad year all round. Norman had got his accounts sorted in good time but was miserable, and fed up and after the Christmas do, he recognised that he probably wouldn't meet anyone new all year. Norman headed home to talk to Neil, his budgie.

Sam, meanwhile, loved life, and was in the habit of saying Yes to everything, really everything. The Yes attitude landed him in Turkey, China, and skiing in the Alps two years back. All he did was say Yes. Sam knew life was short and was going all out to grab it.

Meeting Lisa floored him. Forever he would say yes to lovely Lisa, the love of his life. They did the whole engagement and marriage thing, bought a house, had a family and now he was doing sensible, holding down a fab job at Proctor and Porridge. He applied, they offered him the post and he said Yes, of course.

It was how Sam continued to live. Yes, to induction, Yes to learning, Yes! Yes! Yes! Sam was popular, in the canteen at lunch people wanted to be with him. Sam smiled and said Yes to the offer of a kickaround in the car park, a walk at the weekend, or an extra shift. Sam was a team player.

Sam showed willingness and if ever unsure if yes was the correct reply, he'd say 'Leave it with me' or 'Can I come back to you?' Sam was about to go all out to find a solution. Customers and colleagues, all valued Sam. Great at his job, but better still an engaging, can-do attitude made him a choice for promotion, and an asset to the firm.

Sam was winning at life, Lisa loved him, he really liked his colleagues and saying Yes created happy customers.

Sam continued to knock on Norman's door, knowing one day, one day he might just say, "Come in, yes and let's have a brew!"

Sam and Norman are polar opposites and demonstrate the power and impact of language. Saying yes to everything could land you in trouble, with a list of outstanding, overdue tasks all needed yesterday.

Using words that keep your customers engaged and happy will see you sell more. Simply avoid no, can't, must, should and want and replace with unable, might, could and would like.

PART 2

PROSPECTING

10 Before You Prospect, Maximise Opportunity

Before you begin prospecting, stop and think. Maybe there is an opportunity closer to home? Meet Bella, Colin and, Jude!

Busy Bella

Busy Bella achieved plenty, created opportunities and won business. Busy Bella loved her sales role, was delighted that targets were achievable, and felt the pace made for a fun-packed, exciting day.

Bella, proud to be Queen of New, did not bother with the "keeping in touch with the customers" part of the job. They were customers now, so why bother? Maybe a card at Christmas and a box of mince pies if she was passing, but that was it. Bella had a title to uphold.

When Covid-19 arrived, life changed for Busy Bella. Furloughed, she stopped, took up yoga and meditation, learned about gardening and watched After Life, White Lines and Heist on Netflix - all in a week!

When she went back to work, the setup was different. Clients that had been with Bella for years emailed to cancel. Her pre-book orders fell by 75% in a week. Bella panicked. No one else was losing business so quickly. Conscientious Colin lost nothing, no one, and his pre-book orders remained high. Bella was astounded. This month, Conscientious Colin would make more commission than her. She'd been back just a week, knew about the ninety-day rule, knew exactly how long it took from the first touchpoint to deal done. For the first time since joining the company, she was going to miss Target!

Bella's customers were waving bye-bye, en masse!

Conscientious Colin

Conscientious Colin was methodical. Colin made sure he won new business, but unlike Bella, the accounts won ten years ago remained clients today, mostly with a notable increase in revenue value to the company. Colin was proud of his relationships with his clients and the volume of referrals that he received.

Colin had a system. He knew each client's value and ranked them accordingly, Bronze, Silver, and Gold. He knew how frequently to be in touch with each category and by which method. Gold received weekly calls, emails, and LinkedIn support, backed up with a monthly gift or hand-written card with a small gift, biscuits, a Costa voucher, or a book. Colin tracked the frequency, method, and objective of touchpoints with customers. He stored this information in the Customer Relationship Management system, also noting the personal stuff such as birthdays, dog's name or, favorite singer. Every day, Colins time is blocked for two hours for existing clients.

If ever there was an issue, Colin picked it up and sorted it straight away, communicating back at every step. Recognising the importance of being responsive in creating customer loyalty, Colin excelled at consistently creating happy customers who then generated his referrals.

When post-Covid-19 hit, he was asked by one client to reduce costs. Colin recognised the customer's reasons for this request and happily looked to add value. He explained why they enjoyed working together and highlighted the extras including the saving they were making for the client. Colin excelled at talking value and added it wherever he could.

Colin used to be like Busy Bella, but in the 2008 financial crisis, faced with no pre-booking, he had learned a new way to stay extraordinary in sales. Colin knew that his competitors were knocking on his customers' doors, and in a recession, the knocking was loud. Colin worked hard to ensure those doors stayed firmly shut to anyone except him!

There are many Bella's in business, recognised and applauded for being prospecting Ninjas, hungry for sales, winners at creating new business opportunities. Business development is simply what Bella does. Bella is an asset in companies. At this point Toby looks up, questioning that you just said she was losing sales so how can she be an asset?
- Brilliant question Toby!

Hardcore Bella's, who spend all hours hunting for new business, networking like Ninjas, and using LinkedIn like a pro as well as the other tools in the toolbox, are hard to come by. Prospecting is hard work, requires grit and a thick skin. When you have a Bella, hang on to them. Importantly, support them!

Let us go back in time to make this clearer. In the 1980s, nearly forty years ago, if you wanted to buy something and you were in business, you would visit the golf club and chat with another person in business, (most likely a chap) and see who he suggested. If not the golf club, then the bank manager, or that closed group with a funny handshake. If interested, you'd make a call, set up a meeting and think about making your purchase. Way off deciding, you had others to meet, quotes to collate, and presentations to study in detail before actually making a decision. Maybe a business lunch or two with an expensive bottle of red to cement the decision.

If this is in audio then a record screech would sit well here, as really, that is how it happened! Progress came with the Yellow Pages as a place to find everything and for those that remember the J R Hartley ads, you will recall the one where the older gentleman was looking for a fly-fishing book. How times have changed!

The history lesson is nearly done but is needed for context. Today in business, when you need to make a purchase, you begin by looking at **the thing** online. Your social media knows you looked, so will send more info about **the thing**. You talk to others about how they find **the thing**, study reviews, maybe see a webinar or visit a stand at an exhibition. Then, when you're nearly ready to buy **the thing,** you make contact. You are 60% of the way through the buying process. A salesperson's dream, right? Yes, if they recognise this fact. Many don't and go straight back to explaining when the company began, the size of the team, share the values, culture, and dog policy. Are you still with me? Exactly - an opportunity missed and prospect asleep or gone.

This is when the opportunity can be lost. The prospect, let us call them Ready To Buy Rachel, looks at your website. It is old, screams about Covid causing delays, the latest news post is from 2020, the "Meet the Team" page has faces replaced with silhouettes, the "Contact Us" page form is sending emails to junk and omitting a direct dial or named email.

Then, the prospect calls. Rachel is met with a machine saying, "Your call is important to us". The on-hold music, "So Tired of Waiting" by the Kinks plays, ironic thinks Rachel as she waits and waits. About to hang up, the call is answered, "Hello, no, Bella is not here, call back, she may be here in ten".

Shocker thinks Rachel and googles another company. She'd met Bella. She was switched on, she knew her stuff and he was looking forward to learning more and was open to working with her. Pity!

Bella never knew Rachel called. No one ever knew Rachel called. No one ever measured the missed opportunity. However great the business development people are, without backup and support from everyone in the organisation at all stages of a customer journey, an opportunity will be lost.

Before you invest time and money into prospecting new business, take a look at how you and the whole company deliver extraordinary to your existing clients. Many companies spend time, money and quality training for the sales team and omit to look at the first impression the whole company delivers.

Bella might be brilliant at hunting out new business, but opportunity is lost when prospects independently enquire. Before beginning, going all out to win new, stop a moment and check - if you were looking to work with you, how would those early stages feel?

Every person in your company is a potential ambassador showcasing what you do and how you do it. Everyone in your company could reflect your values and culture. Share warmth, be able to build rapport and as a starting point display great manners. The polite, friendly, fun person that answers the enquiry could lock in the prospect. They could begin a relationship with your company, by listening and showcasing that they listened by taking notes to refer to later, importantly talking about how you frequently help other companies who have similar problems to solve. Making your prospect (who, remember, is 60% ready to buy) feel great about calling and understanding exactly what happens next. A meeting, further call, and diary invite should be sent. The critical part of this call is how the prospect feels when the call ends. Do they feel like they did the right thing by calling and have absolutely no intention of googling, calling or placing a further enquiry with your competitor?

For the moment forget about the big fancy sales processes, slick questioning techniques, stand-out marketing campaigns and super cool promotions. Maximising opportunity when prospects look at you online or make an enquiry is about people, all the people in your company able to build rapport, show empathy and respond quickly. To make prospects and customers feel good falls to everyone.

When Rachel reached out to Bella's company any future business was lost, ignored and gone. How many businesses take time to measure the opportunities they lost?

First Impressions – pre-doing business with you
Try calling your own business. How easy is it to contact you? Who answers? How long does it take? What happens after hours? Are you available when people want to buy or at least find out about what you offer?

Enquire through your website, social media, and other platforms. How long until you are met with a human voice, a real person asking how they can help? How speedy is the reply?

Have a look at your website from a stranger's perspective or maybe ask a stranger to do this part. Watch as they look at your offering. How easy is it for them to access the info they need? Which page is most visited? Meet the Team is often at the top. It's a people thing because we like to know who we are speaking with. Do they look friendly, honest? Do I feel (the emotion thing again) empathy? When we feel empathy, we trust and buy more. There really is a reason why we all go for Heinz Tomato Ketchup and Walkers Crips, the limbic brain is making decisions on how we feel about a brand.

How would a prospect feel about your team, especially if not even visible on your website?

Toby shuffles and comments, "While we're on Meet the Team, I absolutely hate getting my picture taken and usually avoid that". - Seriously, Toby, get over yourself! It's a picture, a moment in time that will be looked at fleetingly for seconds. During those seconds, all 3 for the record, the prospect is not looking at your grey hair, spot or, big nose, they see a person who they can relate to. That's it! For those who value a fab pic, professional shots really are a good idea. The lighting, angle and pose are all worth the investment. If looking to reflect your business as a top drawer, avoid the picture on a car pose or half the wedding photo, and invest in a professional photographer. Thank you, Tim Hardy, for mine!

How is your social media? Many salespeople who are smashing targets without using social media ignore it, after all, they are doing OK, thank you! Companies who have never done the social media thing ignore it too, after all, we have been in business since 1972 and have done OK thank you!

I get it - if it's not broken why fix it? But staying still is a bad idea if you're looking to achieve growth. Be where your customers are! If your customers and prospects are changing how they want to enquire, buy, or use what you offer, then let them. To do that you have to move forward. Is it scary? Yes, sometimes because new software, technology and ways of communication are all immensely fast-paced and have to be learned. Sticking to just your way will see you lose out.

Recently I was enquiring about replacing some software. The new company made it so easy. Try us for free, let us hold your hand as we guide you through, and look at the videos and pointers as you go. The software was superb, notably better than what I had been using. Still, it felt (emotions again) like a big commitment to switch and to invest time in learning about it.

Our emotions drive our decisions! Meet Luddite Larry. Larry was not in favor of moving forward. More likely his position on technology, software and social media was the reverse. He carried a big A4 diary, had the last ten years 'diaries under his desk gathering dust and until recently was doing all right, thank you!

Larry had been in the sales team for over 17 years, so he knew it all, had seen it all and felt that there was absolutely no need to change anything. Larry was old school, happy to do things the old way, pen, paper, and the deal in cash. All this social media stuff was killing time, showing casing your identity, potential fraud and ultimately for teenagers!

Larry, who for the past few years has kept his head firmly in the sand, began to get twitchy. The new boy was able to get himself in front of some big companies and close business. Larry was losing his grip on being Number One. You can read more about Larry in future chapters.

There are many Larry's who have achieved greatness in their day. If, however, your prospects are researching you ahead of being in touch and remember, are 60% ready to buy, then you're not being where they are looking is a bad idea. You could be on LinkedIn reflecting you and your brand as top quality, Number One.

Toby's hand goes up. "I hear you, but I really don't have time for this social media stuff."
- Toby, you don't have time for social media stuff or just don't have time.

We all have plenty of time, 24 hours in any one day. How we use our time is a training module all of its own. However, in sales where, guess what, salespeople are paid to sell, making time for social media is key if you plan to use all your prospecting tools. A little-known fact, over 80% of business-to-business leads originate from or involve people looking at LinkedIn. You could be there or not. LinkedIn is a brilliant platform that enables you to showcase yourself, share content, learn, and nurture relationships. It takes **time,** planned into your week, maybe an hour or two to engage and build familiarity.

Using your time wisely to deliver a return is always a good idea. Given that consistent prospecting delivers a return if completed using all the tools, then it might be worth **Time** blocking an appointment with yourself to do social media. Chances are your competitors will be doing this already.

Imagine if right now your competitors were talking to your top clients and have been exchanging conversations for months. Your competitors have been watching their video content, learning from their posts, and have just signed up to attend their next big event. Would that be OK? The worst part is that they meet your top clients by accessing your network through your, not so little, black book. How does it feel? Unfair, wrong, and simply not on?
- Toby, your competitors made **time** to be on social media!

Do you recall that earlier I mentioned J R Hartley and the Yellow Pages? LinkedIn is similar in that it is a huge professional directory for businesses. If you go to Google or LinkedIn the likelihood is that links to your LinkedIn will appear. If you're there, in those first few seconds what impression do you make?

It is unlikely the receptionist, driver and service engineer will use LinkedIn the same way as account managers or new business development teams. Being found for what you do, and reflecting professionalism is a good idea. In the same way, your Meet the Team page works. Be found with a professional, friendly picture, link to your company and have easy, clear contact info. Take off the link to your personal Facebook, home email and date of birth. This is *business*, not what your cat had for breakfast, how fab your holiday was or, how you bought the new Bond film. It is *business* and as such can reflect your business well, or not.

Remember Ready To Buy Rachel who had met Bella and was less than impressed when calling her company? Rachel was in the area of Bella's HQ and decided to drive past. She pulls over and notices the cigarette shelter is strewn with cigarette butts on the floor. The raised planters are full of rubbish, cans, plastic bottles, and a half-eaten sandwich. A seagull swoops down for his tea. There is the company logo on a sign propped up in a window. From the car, the visitor can make out the lists of companies on the doorbell pad - but not the one they were hoping to visit. The hanging basket displays dead-looking flowers, and the weathered plastic box tree below screams tacky. The car park is rammed. The visitor's space has the company delivery van in it and a Deliveroo bike parked up against the wall. Maybe they won't pop in after all.

If I were to visit your company what would my first impression be? Does the postcode on Google take me to the right place? Is parking easy? Does everything about the first minute or two of visiting your company suggest that you will look after my business? Do you make people feel welcome (it's there again - emotion)? Would I feel like I wanted to stay?

Years ago, I visited an accounting firm as a follow-up call after an event. On arrival, the sign created especially for me said "Welcome Sally Roberts". Wow, I felt special! The firm just took a few minutes to print my name on an A4 piece of paper and put it in the car park. That first impression has lasted for years! A pretty good return on investment.

Exercise

Walk through your premises as though you were a stranger and experience the first impression people have when visiting your company. Think security, barriers, instructions...

Visiting a respected insurance company once, I was shown into the waiting room. It happened to be next to the open plan office where a young lady was sharing, at volume, the events from her weekend out, and she had been out out!! She shared, everything! It was detailed, graphic and massively inappropriate for an office supposedly taking calls. The impression was clearly a fun team but slightly unaligned with the image the CEO and marketing team were keen to portray.

When people visit your company, where do they wait? Worth your while walking through, as though you were a stranger. If there are opportunities, it would be a good idea to change things. Remember, a piece of A4 saying welcome created a phenomenal return!

11 A Prospecting Mindset

"Prospecting is easy", said no one – ever!

Have you heard the one about the salesperson that hit a target by doing nothing? No, because it does not happen.

Being in sales and starting with absolutely no accounts, a brand-new territory and no one in your network is a scary place to be. Looking at an empty pipeline, no account history, and an empty order book equally so.

You have two choices, panic and run or get gritty and begin prospecting. The thrill of having it all to go at is exciting and ignites a fire in rare salespeople. It is time to create a strategy and importantly a mindset that will see you go all out to win new business, create a network, and fill the order book.

But first and this is a massive first, given there are only so many hours in the day, you need to be efficient with yours. So, who are you prospecting for? What does your ideal new client and business look like?

Let's take a step back before heading into the field in your company car, to knock on doors and showcase your face-to-face prospecting talent. Whom are you wanting to work with?

Prospecting with precision is critical if you are to win business fast. Wasting time talking to lovely people who are more than happy to pass the time of day yet have no need for what you sell, is a poor use of your time. Knowing your ideal client, their details, company size, portfolio value, location, and the decision maker's name is the beginning.

Understanding what value your company could bring and the problems you could solve offers the opportunity to create the next step. Only when you know your ideal referral can you ask for it?

First, an exercise in prospecting that sits neatly alongside marketing. It's about knowing who you want to sell to and being able to recognise them. Bring out your inner detective and create a profile of your ideal prospect. In training the drawing begins with a picture of the ideal client's business on the left of the page. The building, turnover, number of employees, existing problems noted and title of decision maker to target. All guesswork but it will ensure you are effective with your time when using your prospecting toolbox. Making time now to understand and recognise your ideal client will see you minimise the time in the future chatting to a dog groomer or reiki healer who is unlikely to be looking for a £20,000 tech solution any time soon. Once the business is noted, next to the person.

Toby was textbook and asks the same question as many. "The person, Sally, isn't that a bit odd? Why do I want to profile the person when I have a clear picture of the ideal business?"

Toby's question is common and expected. Many sales training courses talk about being efficient and knowing the business and less if any discuss the person. Here's a missed opportunity especially as we understand decisions to buy are made with the limbic brain, the limbic brain belonging to a person, your prospect. We know that people buy people so it is a massive advantage if you have a profile of the person, you will be targeting.

Back to drawing, this time the decision maker, on the right-hand side of the page. A fun picture with a note of the name, job title and their likely age, interests outside of work, where they will go networking, which exhibitions they are likely to attend, possible ambition and what keeps him or her awake at night.

Arguably this too is all guesswork and that is alright. Giving thought to the prospect ahead of meeting them will see you at an advantage. Building empathy is far easier if you have noted their interest in cars, award ceremonies or, health and well-being issues.

Being able to connect with the person is a doddle when you can recognise them and have an idea of what they might be like. This trick puts you ahead of the competition.

Great! Now you know to whom you are prospecting and importantly why. Understanding the solutions, you can bring means it's time to begin.

On completion of the prospecting profile training, a task is to deliver your prospecting target list for the next 90 days. Make your list, begin with thirty do they fit your ideal?

If only it was this easy! Often when sales reps begin and are new in the post they go all out, 100mph and hit the phones. Their call rate is through the roof, tenacity displayed and enthusiasm in abundance. Then it happens, the slow down, the "No" leads to hesitancy when next picking up the phone, booking a meeting or making, well, any calls at all. The initial flourish is abandoned as supplied data runs out and the reality dawns. Consistent prospecting is hard work.

It is hard work, and consistency is the most amazing quality a prospecting salesperson can bring. A flourish of activity, however brilliant, won't put money in the till. Consistent commitment to prospecting will. Regardless of the circumstances, finding time, making time, and blocking time to prospect will see you create success. Prospecting is your must-do job, critical to success and you are not a tree so drive your day and own it.

Let me introduce Every Excuse Ed! You will have met Ed. Most salespeople recognise him and often relate to his many traits frequently seen in poor sales teams.

Every Excuse, Ed did exactly what his nickname said. He made every excuse to avoid prospecting. The excuse list was long and fueled by a negative mindset. He was terrified of hearing "No". If a no was received, inside he cried, wilted, and wanted to run, taking it personally, thinking it was a criticism of him. Overthinking the reasons why the no landed wasted so much time. The no added to his negative mindset and was shared with whoever would listen which only made the "o last longer in his mind and provided a massive excuse not to move forward. In prospecting, no will happen. Ed was still so absorbed in the "No," from yesterday that he had not called anyone or done any proactive activity towards a sale today, for fear of another, you guessed it, "No"!

When it rained Ed believed no one would buy. It was raining so after all, why would anyone want to take his call? When the sun shone Ed avoided the phone recognising that everyone would be sunbathing or at least outside enjoying the weather rather than wanting to take his call. If windy, foggy, warm or, just flat, Every Excuse Ed found the weather a superb excuse for not dialing. His latest excuse was a serious lack of incoming leads, no one to call because no one gave him people to call. Ed was missing by a mile the fact that his new sales job involved prospecting. If having to dig for excuses, then marketing would be next in his firing line. The company website was terrible, the brochure not colorful enough and the latest flyers not saying the right thing. Ed blamed the economy for no incoming calls and the reason why no one would want to speak to him. He knew that with a recession close no one would want a sales call. Ed understood if a prospect did take a call, they would have no money and that would bring a no. He blamed wars, elections, and pandemics for doing absolutely nothing.

Ed's worst traits were what we call the 3 Ps. He would talk on repeat to anyone that would listen about what he might do today, tomorrow maybe if only the weather was better. Ed had *Procrastination* down to a fine art. The notion of beginning was talked about plenty but never actually happened. There were many wasted hours, weeks, and months of procrastinating. *Perfectionism* was Ed's next reason for not doing anything. Time to tidy his desk before picking up the phone, perfect his script, pitch, and presentation, make a perfect brew and then rearrange his desk drawers before sorting out the filing cabinet. The bonsai tree could benefit from a clip and then next, maybe vacuum the floor. A tidy desk, and a tidy mind were taken to the extreme. It was learned as a child when cleaning his bedroom before even looking at his school homework. Then there was overthinking! Finally, *Paralysis* from analysis, over-analysis! With good reason ironically Ed thought the team were talking about him. Watching a hushed conversation in the corner of the next-door office, two people whispering, Ed was sure they were talking about him, his lack of sales calls maybe. He wanted to lean in and hear the exact words. He then spent time sharing what he was thinking might have been said about him by the two people whom he did not know that worked in another office.

STOP! Too much and so visible in poor-performing sales teams. It is easy to want perfection or put excuses in our path. Ed was extreme albeit relatable. If you're planning to be a winning, prospecting superstar performer like Freya learn how not to prospect, avoid a poor prospecting mindset, and understand the failings in how Ed operates.

Freya was the polar opposite of Ed. If you find or create a Freya hang on to them because they are rare. Freya's number one rule was understanding her pipeline needed constant attention. She was always looking to fill up her pipe with potential opportunities and so allocated time to prospect using all the tools in her prospecting toolbox. Never complacent, when a prospect converted to a sale, she kept her foot on the gas and put more opportunities in her path.

Freya learned a long time ago, having read Jeb Blount's book on Fanatical Prospecting that understanding your strike rate is

crucial. Rule number one of sales is, to know your numbers.
When Freya had 30 prospects in her pipeline, with a strike rate of 1 in 10, it was 10%. Freya knew that by closing 1 in 10 the pipe is reduced by 10, therefore needs to increase by 10 new prospects.

In training, this equation is shared and usually guessed incorrectly with teams suggesting that 29 opportunities are left in the pipe. If your strike is accurate, then you have received 9 "No's" before getting a "Yes" then adding new prospects to the pipeline is a good idea.

The prospects who declined your offering because of timing, don't need any or many reasons, for now they are a "No". Keeping on at them, pestering, sending a PDF, brochure or calling a further twenty times will annoy a future prospect. They said "No" and that is unlikely to change in the near future if you get their backup. Instead, and this is the key message, keep topping up your pipeline with new quality opportunities if you are to win new business.

Freya displayed many fabulous prospecting traits. She was positive and spoke about how she had achieved her target, was a winner and fed her brain the good stuff. Her mindset was that of a winner. She had an absolute belief that she had achieved and as such went all out to deliver. Freya understood that being flexible was key, networking, and meeting prospects at their most suitable times whether early starts, after work, during lunch, or even at the gym. Being flexible saw, her earn opportunities that many ignored or thought silly.

Freya was effective with her time, understanding the importance of targeting your ideal prospect and having meetings noted in the CRM. Data was her friend and not viewed as a slog. Task reminders to call, email or send a birthday card opened doors that others might find firmly shut. Her relentless approach, looking and finding ways to create an opportunity ensured she was top of the prospecting charts. Others were shocked when she booked a meeting or call with a perceived tricky person to get hold of. Freya smiled inside, calm, and motivated. She was also fiercely competitive, wanted to be the top dog, win salesperson of the month and year, and enjoy the big bonus. Keeping Freya ahead of the game in part was the volume of relevant audiobooks and podcasts she listened to. Driving to calls, and getting ready for the day, all with Alexa playing sales tips, winner wisdom and successful sales stories from leaders. Freya had no time for news or negative things, she had a bonus to earn.

Freya was more than capable of driving her day, booking good prospecting time. She valued her productive time and used it wisely. She also relished praise, recognition and a well done! Not a big flash award, just a well-done, thank-you or a weekly check-in. Freya made the prospecting role look easy. It wasn't easy. Consistent prospecting is tough, and the praise and recognition boosted Freya and fed her winning mindset.

I was like Freya when I was working on the radio. Top biller at the station and in the country, I was punching high and the figures (viewed by all) earned me a winning reputation. It was early February and the MD from the sister station was visiting our MD and sales team.

He stopped to say hello to the sales team and asked how we were doing with Target for the month. My reply was, "Target is in the bag, done now, looking at March."
He was stunned and replied, "Done, in the system, all booked and secure?"
"Still to go in the system but yes, done and secure."
He sat down, disbelieving.

He thought I was arrogant, big for my boots claiming to have hit the target so soon. Maybe I was a little, there is after all a fine line between confidence and arrogance. Yet in my head, I had only ever delivered success. Hit target achievement for 25 months on the trot and February would be the same, a win. Because I would always crack on and prospect, find opportunities, delight clients, and deliver a fabulous customer experience that led to referrals and opportunities to up and cross-sell.

The visiting MD remained perplexed. His team never achieved, struggled to get through the month and blamed most things for this. Strikingly, as a team leader, his mindset was less than winning.

To be brilliant at constantly prospecting requires you to drive your day, do the difficult tasks and block time to prospect. Salespeople are paid to sell, and it begins with precise, consistent, positive mindset prospecting.

Wayne (or **Wing it Wayne** as he is known) and his polar opposite Olly, (**On It Olly**) are characters whose sales journey I share throughout prospecting and sales training. Recognising where Wayne gets it wrong, and Olly right reinforces the importance of consistent prospecting.

Wing it Wayne was a lad, a geezer, a fella who liked the banter, the laughter, and the ladies! Wing it Wayne took playing it cool to the extreme, he was so laid back he was pretty much horizontal.

Wayne's approach to sales was lacking drive. He knew he could sell, people would meet him and want to buy, wouldn't they? He was confident with bells on, but it was to be his downfall.

Wing it Wayne could not be bothered with prospecting, that was for losers or so he thought. When taken to task about his diary and a distinct lack of time blocking, Wayne blamed other departments for booking training, the economy for delaying people wanting to buy, the marketing department for not providing brochures, IT for not creating enough incoming leads, the weather for rain, snow, or sun - it was simply the wrong weather.

On the odd occasion, Wayne recognised he had no choice but to prospect because the boss who sat opposite him was in. Wayne tidied his desk and drawers and called his new girlfriend to share how he was paranoid that the IT department had it in for him and how everyone else got the leads. He talked to her about many things for at least forty minutes, maybe that could be logged as a sales call - help his call duration? The next call was to his Mum, then his Nan.

When Wayne did cold call, if answered by a dragon, the evil, awful gatekeeper, he was abrupt, ill-mannered and would say, "It's Wayne from the IT Tech Company. He wants to talk to me, Luv, put me through doll!" Funny, his Mum always replied with a smile when he called her "doll". This awful gatekeeper invariably hung up!

Social media and LinkedIn for business, not a chance! Wayne just watched Tik Tok, maybe he could log that as social media prospecting. When asked to email a prospect, a one-liner did the trick although he never received a reply.

Networking was the new thing, that, and exhibitions. Wayne thought he would go for the free bar, the beer on expenses, that was a win! After networking or an exhibition, he would be back on with the day job. Maybe time to tidy his desk again!

Three months in and his sales manager was talking about a ninety-day rule, whatever that was. Wayne was baffled, his sales were zero, commission zero and pipeline empty! Wayne wondered why HR and his sales manager wanted a word!

Olly was nicknamed On It Olly for good reason. He was on it!

Olly knew it was all about keeping his pipeline full, never taking your foot off the gas, keeping on it daily and being consistent! Weekly, his diary was packed with power hours, networking events, webinars, and social media.

Olly was King of the cold call, nurturing relationships with Ethel, calling, building rapport, asking for help, and finding himself put through to the decision-maker with relative ease. Wayne used social media to source prospects, then to follow, watch, interact and in time reach out. On social media, if stuck, using Lusha or Zoom Info to find contact details worked a treat. How cool that this software was available to make his life easier, thought Olly! His success was staggering, it was a slow burn, but Olly knew that big fish move slowly.

He enjoyed networking and taking it seriously. He would eat before the meeting with the intention to speak freely with as many people as possible who looked like his ideal prospect. He knew it was not a selling situation so was relaxed in his approach, talking about them, engaging in curiosity and quality conversation. Afterwards, he always followed up with a LinkedIn Connection, a coffee, or a call.

When attending exhibitions as a guest or exhibitor, Olly always had a goal. He had planned and he was ready. He had seen the guest list and knew what his measure of success would be. Occasionally he sent a backup email mentioning problems his prospects shared and showcased how his IT Tech company could help and the results they could bring. His response was good, especially for these emails. This approach combined with referrals worked well for Olly. "Just ask!" was his motto.

Well before the ninety days, Olly was closing business, his activity was huge, meetings, calls, events, and the result - ££ £s, sales, dollar! Olly had calculated his commission and smiled, knowing it was going towards a Porsche.

Olly loved this job - work hard and you get rewarded! Olly had been invited to meet the MD and HR, something about the employee of the month. "Nice touch," thought On It Olly. "Must wear the lilac suit!

12 Make Time To Prospect

Prospecting Takes Time!

Did you hear about the salesperson who had the best-ever prospecting toolbox and sold nothing, nada, nil?

If you don't make time to prospect, it won't happen. Life, meetings, debriefs and a whole load of "very important" stuff will overtake prospecting unless you prioritise and time block.

A sad but common story. Companies recruit salespeople, put them in roles with quality data, and fantastic CRM, sign them up for networking opportunities, and provide a phone, a laptop and a car. The expectation is that armed with all the prospecting tools the salesperson will use them and sales will follow.

Salespeople are paid to sell and should be enabled to do this. The responsibility lies with the salesperson to not be a tree but to own their prospecting day. Clear targets from day one help. Targets focused on activity, calls, meetings, networking attended, not financial not yet that is for 90 days.

The 90-day rule is huge in sales. It can vary across sectors according to the length of time a sales decision or buying cycle can take. The 90 days rule is pretty accurate and definitely effective.

The foundations of the 90-day rule come from the understanding that certain events happen every year, such as Christmas, Easter, summer holidays and more. On It Olly knew this and planned his prospecting activity accordingly.

Wing It Wayne however was guaranteed to say, "Oh it always goes quiet around Christmas, no one ever buys in the summer holidays and everyone is off over Easter." Recognise this approach to prospecting? It is common in failing sales teams across the world. Using the world calendar as a reason not to prospect.

Successful teams understand that events happen annually, so Christmas is not a surprise, Easter is planned for and school holidays are factored in. The school will break up for holidays, Easter and Christmas will happen and business will not stop. You can, and many often do, but business stays moving.

Wing it Wayne, cousin to every Excuse Ed, used Christmas as an excuse to put his feet up from about mid-December when the private schools broke up. He might, at a push, begin to look again at prospecting in the second week of January when all schools returned. Nearly four weeks with no prospecting activity, all because of Christmas! Wayne knew his December prospecting targets would be impossible to hit so did nothing and blamed the season.

On It Olly was on it from the beginning of the new year before that really. Olly knew his targets for money and activity in good time, often annually. He worked backwards, splitting his annual activity target across the weeks he would be working. This allowed for his holiday and any ad hoc away days. Olly added on insurance usually 10% to allow for cancelled appointments, wifi not working, and exhibitions cancelled. A recent pandemic proved to Olly that pivoting and insurance was a good idea.

When Olly and Wayne first joined the company their annual activity targets were the same. A crude division by 52 weeks as calculated by Wayne meant he need to complete 5 face-to-face meetings a week. A breeze thought Wayne at first glance.

Olly viewed the 260 face-to-face meetings differently. Adding on insurance 260 + 10% = 286, then dividing by 45, the number of planned working weeks, allowing for bank holidays and maybe slower days. On It Olly calculated 286 face-to-face divided by 46 weeks meant he needed to book 6.2 a week or 25 a month. With this in mind, Olly went all out from day one filling his diary with quality appointments months in advance. Add in a dollop of efficiency around journey planning and prospects visiting him at HQ and Olly's activity target was achieved in good time. The opposite in approach was Wayne who scrambled around trying to book an appointment for next week, sounding desperate knowing that he was already two weeks behind so promising to drive 300 miles to Glasgow for a meeting with a dog groomer. Wayne was just happy to have an appointment!

The most important factor when talking about effective prospecting is consistency. You have to understand that every minute you take your foot off the gas will catch you out, usually 90 days later. When talking with a salesperson who is struggling, stuck, and failing to understand why this month is so tricky, the "yes's" dried up and no one is buying. The first question is not about right now but the ninety days previous.

It is easy to predict that salespeople who stop prospecting over Christmas will find the ripple effect lands in March. When stopping prospecting over Easter watch out for a quiet July and as for the summer holidays watch out for a less than fruitful November. Prospecting requires a consistent approach. Effective, consistent prospecting means filling your working week with prospecting activity to generate meetings, calls and just coffees. Sometimes of the year might require more grit and tenacity, so real salespeople understand that and dig deep. They win results, they call when others don't, post when social media channels look quiet; they get through and make inroads when others have their feet up because it is Christmas! Doing nothing will get you nothing. Ineffective, sporadic prospecting will lead to ineffective, sporadic poor prospecting activity and few if any sales.

On It Olly knew to expect slow days and that he would be taking a holiday, so he chose to up his activity on the days that he was working. The brilliant win is, Olly can have his holiday knowing target achievement will happen because Olly planned his days to achieve.

On occasions, companies recruit a new salesperson for business development, provide all the prospecting tools and then take the new recruit away from prospecting. Sounds silly, right? Maybe you recognise this scenario?

Imagine a new salesperson, who comes in hungry passionate and keen to get on and sell. The company book compulsory meetings in key selling times. A Health and Safety meeting, a company brief and an HR seminar, whatever that is, have landed in your new, hungry salesperson's diary. As they are new and keen not to rock the boat, they accept all this and suddenly time is taken from them. Meetings about meetings that lead to more meetings. The salesperson is then given tasks, maybe existing accounts. This takes up even more of their time. Time spent not prospecting! If companies want salespeople to sell, they must empower them to do just that. Let them drive their day and make their targets about the activity.

Time blocking is brilliant for all salespeople. How does your diary look? If prospecting, is it full of networking three times a week, exhibitions, follow-up coffees, face-to-face meetings, account reviews, calls, more calls and power hours, time allocated for social media, gifts and email?

If you are blocking time with yourself, then you commit to a diary packed with prospecting activity. If you're not, then chances are you won't, allowing distractions, admin, birthday chat and all that stuff to take your eye off what you have been hired to do.

Winning salespeople make time and commit to consistent prospecting. Winning salespeople, with this approach to prospecting sell more.

13 The Toolbox

Prospecting is a mix, there is no magic bullet. Use all the tools in the prospecting toolbox to build familiarity, awareness and keep them front of mind.

We are often sold on 'Easy' and 'New'. Who wouldn't love an easy new approach to prospecting? We spend thousands on doing a LinkedIn course, buying some super sales software, or investing in a one-day super sales programme. Teams jump up and down saying, "Yee-ha!" spending money on the day, enjoying a hotel lunch believing that tomorrow they will be a prospecting ninja - after just one day!

Oh, dear! There is no easy route to effective prospecting. There is no single tool in the prospecting toolbox to create phenomenal success. Prospecting is a careful mix of all the tools.

Understanding the 7 tools in your toolbox is a good beginning.

Unquestionably the best tool in your toolbox is referrals. This is what your customer experience strives to deliver and sits outside your sales process. The power of a referral, as will be mentioned in step 11, is wonderful. More and more referrals will see your sales soar. You do, however, need to build a trusted network and find clients to delight before you will receive any referrals.

There are other tools mentioned briefly here. These will be explored in detail in the following chapters.

Networking is a superb way to meet your ideal prospect if, and it is a big if, you are networking where they are. Being efficient with your time and investment matters, especially when networking. Networking events are like music gigs, some events you will love, others less so. If you are new to your post then try lots, ask for suggestions and immerse yourself. When you have visited many, several times, decide and commit to the ones you enjoy, that can deliver benefits and where you have something to offer so you can pay it forward. Most importantly remember that networking is not selling. Being a Today Only Tony, handing out a flyer, or talking at people with a one-day-only special offer will see you lonely and unsuccessful.

Exhibitions are a sensational place to win opportunities if you do it right. Decision makers who want what you have to offer are in the same building, excited to see new innovations. If exhibiting, avoid arriving late with a tablecloth, brochure, and free pen. Sitting down behind a table, talking to no one, and having absolutely no follow-up plan frequently sees exhibition opportunities wasted. Eating lunch, making a call, or showcasing a stinking hangover all deliver little return on investment.

Social media is a win when building familiarity and awareness. Share how you help others and the solutions you bring. Post about your culture, brand, and the fun you have. Doing this consistently will showcase you beautifully for all the right reasons. When your social media network is made up of people you want to prospect, they will see what you do and are more than likely to call you over a stranger or better still your competition.

Call. Cold, warm, hot just call. Deservedly calling has a place in the toolbox and yet it sends shivers down spines. Just call, not in a staged sales voice that sounds cringey, desperate and fake. Be yourself, 'call Ethel', build and nurture the contact and importantly, when you land a call with the decision maker, be prepared, make it count and follow a process. Calling works and is made easier by blending with other tools.

Email is often viewed as the savior of prospecting. Why call when you can email? Here is a big why, emails are mostly deleted, unread and ineffective. Even with tricks to see emails opened, an email is just an email and unlikely to win you an opportunity. Spam, firewalls, and blockers are great at preventing your brilliant email from getting through. If it does arrive and your prospect has no clue who you are or, even worse they think you're selling, stand by for delete.

Text with caution. Text is more likely to see a speedy response but be careful. It is viewed as personal and texting someone you don't know is like demanding a conversation with a stranger in a bar. Most likely your number will be blocked.

Webinars during the pandemic were a lifeline when prospecting, especially if you could see who was in attendance. It is not a boom, wow tool, it is a little complementary tool that can deliver wins and is a part of the mix.

Your prospecting toolbox is a gift to all business development salespeople. Knowing which tool to use and when takes time and practice. Consider your prospecting plan for the next 90 days. When do you plan to network, call, email, use social media and go to, or showcase at an exhibition? By committing to the plan, with time blocked in your diary and driving your prospecting activity you will begin to create an opportunity that leads nicely into your sales process - or certainly just a coffee.

Of note and worth a mention here is the follow-up. Being a prospecting superstar, meeting and creating opportunities is absolutely wasted if you do not follow up.

14 Referrals

To Be Referred you need to be referable.

The Referral, is your number one tool in the prospecting toolbox. The final part of a sales process and something that happens naturally when you consistently deliver an extraordinary customer experience.

The referral is often ignored, stepped over and worse, misunderstood. It is met with a sigh or a squirm. When training I will ask who requests referrals and the looks are those of a guilty child who ignores their homework. 'I know I should but....'

A true story to make my point! My network is good, and full of excellent businesspeople, leaders, advisors and importantly decision makers. It was not given to me, nor did it appear on day one of being in business. It has taken years to acquire, time spent meeting, learning and sometimes just having a coffee. The result is a network that I treasure and am proud of.

There is value in introducing people who could help each other, keeping an ear out on behalf of your network and when applicable introducing them. Often the more you pay it forward the more it comes back, usually when least expected.

One time, someone who recognised the value in my network (let's call him Wayne) mentioned it to someone else who I happened to know. Ok, cards on the table, merely knowing someone and meeting them does not mean by default I will share my network. If I don't know you well, why would I recommend you? Truly knowing someone takes time, building like and trust - yep back to the limbic brain. Trust and relationships are fragile and require nurture and not an introduction to every new person you happen to meet everywhere.

Back to the story. This person, a dog groomer, meets Wayne. Wayne had been told about the value of referrals and also to fill his diary. That is why having been prompted (or arguably instructed) by his manager, he was having a coffee with a dog groomer. Wayne knew the dog groomer was unlikely to buy what he sold, and he was unlikely to need thousands of glossy print brochures, but at least Wayne had what he thought to be an appointment in his diary. Nor did Wayne have a dog or know of any that need grooming, still it would keep his manager off his case for a day at least.

Wayne enjoyed the coffee, cake, and very long meeting. He dragged it out so he could go home straight after, it was 3 pm after all. When talking about dogs, breeds and football, the other person mentioned sales and training. That he had met me and that my network was huge and packed with decision-makers who always said yes. Wayne began listening, put his coffee down and asked more. Wayne realised we knew each other as we had met at an event. Excellent thought Wayne and he mentioned to the dog groomer that he'd be in touch. Coffee down, Wayne got up, thanked the dog groomer and was off. No mention of paying or going halves, he was off. All opportunities to influence with reciprocation are ignored.

The message soon arrived.

Hey Sally, how's it going? Just sat with The Dog Groomer and he mentioned you have a little black book of contacts to share!

No elaboration, that was the message. I mention it when training as a 'how not to'. One lady was horrified. Asking the room how they would reply she said, "You told him to get lost, right?" She was even more horrified to hear my response, "You're absolutely right, my black book is huge and of course, I will share it with you, Wayne."

Wayne would have received the message, smiled and been so happy that decision-makers who say yes to everything would one day be coming his way all because of a coffee and a message. Wayne would be happy that in his mind I agreed to help. Wayne would also never follow up. He didn't. As it goes, they rarely do. If he had, I would have helped, not by passing over all my contacts, but I'd have helped.

Asking for referrals the right way matters. Many companies cringe, recoil, or look away at the suggestion of asking their existing client base and network for a referral in case it makes them look desperate. One company I worked with was initially genuinely concerned that they might be perceived as desperate and that asking for referrals could suggest they might be in trouble.

Daniel, a smart entrepreneur with London and Leeds offices met me and was exasperated when it came to referrals. He knew the value and wanted his call centre teams to ask all their customers in every call for a referral, just to ask. If they asked, they won a £20 M&S voucher – still, they did not ask. Daniel was beside himself and did not understand why. Nerves, low confidence, a want to not be rude plus little understanding of why referrals mattered, all contributed to the teams simply not asking. When his team understood how to ask and importantly the language to use, change began, and vouchers were won. Asking for referrals is a good idea, better still asking in the right way at the right time if you want to be referred.

In training, I tell the story of Richard. Allow me to set the screen. I am 16, big hair, high school and Wham are key factors in life. As is Richard. We are friends but secretly I think he is gorgeous, blue eyes to get lost in, a blue bomber jacket and Farrah trousers. If you're my age you will get this. The thing is I wanted not to be in the friend zone. I wanted Richard to be my boyfriend, but could not utter the words "Will you go out with me, will you be my boyfriend, could we go on a date?" It was beyond awkward, cringingly embarrassing.

With hindsight, Richard had a thing for my best friend of the time, Rachel. Rachel was 5 '6" blonde and beautiful. Richard probably wanted to say to Rachel, "Will you go out with me, will you be my girlfriend, could we go on a date?" He never did. It would have been beyond awkward, cringingly embarrassing. Being sixteen was tricky. Ironically Rachel only had eyes for George Michael and that was never going to work out for obvious reasons, not known then. Thank you, Wham and George, for creating a fabulous soundtrack to my teenage years.

There is a reason I share this story. When you are 16 being awkward, embarrassed, and shying away from asking for what you want makes total sense. When you are in business though, especially in a business development role or looking for growth, then asking for referrals is a must. Politely get over the awkwardness and get on with asking the right way.

Oddly something strange happens when you begin and continue to ask for referrals. You begin to be referred. Funny that ask and you shall receive, often from the most unexpected source. It is a little like earl grey tea, with sweeteners, or vegetarian options.

Another story from training, I ask the room if anyone is vegetarian. Usually, a hand or two goes up, excellent. Those people by default have just become part of the story. Say, Amy. Amy is invited to my house for a summer bbq. She arrives an hour or so in and the bbq is laden with meat, sausages, ribs, steak, you name it, laden. A few wines in and a warm welcome for Amy and Alex her partner. Guided to the bbq and asking what they'd like, Amy shares that she is veggie. Do WHAT!! Veggie, I had no clue, there is nothing remotely veggie on this bbq other than coleslaw. Creatively I rustle up beans on wholemeal toast for Amy and she is happy.

Alex and Amy hit it off with our friends and family so the next time they come over I am prepared and this time an M&S Veggie special is served. The third time, the Jamie Oliver cookbook is out, and I am rustling up a veggie curry that would impress anyone!

The story is fiction, rustling up anything is very un-Sally. The message however is loud. When people know what you want, they will if they like you, provide it. Think of the aunt who only drinks earl grey tea, and the builders who take sugar. When we know what people want because as human beings, we are nice, we want to provide it. If your clients (who for the record love working with you and know that you love working with them) are informed that in the next two years, you are looking to grow and work with more companies that look like them and value quality. Guess what, they will refer, and your customers become your sales force.

But take note, if you keep quiet, shy away and, don't ask, then sit back and wait for absolutely no referrals to come your way.

Time for a note on leads. A lead is not a referral, it is a lead. There is a distinction that is sometimes overlooked.

In the early days of being in business, a colleague who was keen to support my success called frequently with leads. "Sally I am at this exhibition and the chaps at this incredible-looking stand are, well, simply awful. They are sitting behind the table, talking to each other, and ignoring all this business potential walking straight by. They needy you Sally, they really need you." Next time, "Sally can you talk, I have just had lunch at this fab hotel and the service was shocking, the receptionist stared at us on arrival and then pointed to the restaurant. No warmth, empathy, or care, it got worse Sally, a real shame because the food was delicious. Sally, they need you and fast."

The lovely colleague, who remains a part of my network, had the best of intentions, they were looking out for an opportunity.

However, spending time chasing leads is hard work, hard work. A referral, now that is a gem and it's worthy of note that referrals are 80% likely to result in a sale. You see a lead is not a referral. My colleague sent plenty of leads my way. A referral, however, - now that feels good!

A referral comes with an introduction and praise. The email introducing you, the story about what you have achieved and maybe a link to your reviews or recommendations. Then the suggestion that a meeting can only benefit both of you. Numbers and emails were exchanged. That is a referral. That is a great feeling. No cold call, warming up Ethel, networking and exhibitions bypassed, your customer has put you in front of your future client who needs what you do. The lowest-hanging fruit, the speedier route to a sale is a referral.

That feeling, like in the World Cup, when Harry Kane scores the winning goal …. or the Friday feeling after the first sip of Malbec from the right glass. That winning at-life feeling! In business that winning feeling comes with a referral, call, email, or introduction. It's the dream. You have been introduced and referred - the hard work of prospecting, done for you. Someone you know like, and trust has referred you. You are 80% of the way to a done deal. Most odd, when that feeling is so great, that so few people in business ask for referrals. Referral should be the number one tool in your prospecting toolbox.

Salespeople smile and embrace the message before the most critical part of this equation is mentioned. To be referred, you must be referable. Toby is back, "Sally, my business is excellent of course it will be referable" Toby has a point, he usually does but the reply sees him take note. "Toby, you are right, your business product or service is excellent, but it is you that needs referring, not your fancy website, logo, or product Toby, you." It is back to the limbic brain, the emotional decision, do I like, and do I trust

Toby - then and only then will you be referred. It helps if you have asked for referrals.
To be referred you must be referable.
"How do you become referable," Toby asks.
- Doing the right thing Toby, delighting clients, going all out and over-delivering, leaving your customers blown away by the experience of working with you, having you in their team.

It can take time. But a speedy route to a referral is looking after (with bells on) all your existing clients. When they rave about you, and the experience of working with you, then your clients become your sales force which is a huge win because their opinion about your business is trusted way more than you saying how good you are.

In training a photographer named Tim Hardy is on a slide highlighting people whom I refer because they are referable. Tim is lovely, kind and an excellent photographer. I have enjoyed referring him many times, knowing when he meets his future clients they will be just as impressed. Tim is unassuming, polite, and absolutely not an all-out, loud, salesperson. He does however spend time understanding clients 'needs and then delivers the result, fantastic pictures. He does a brilliant job. When, post-event, you're thinking the pictures might arrive later that week, surprise, the link is sent in just a few hours. Your clients are thrilled, the pictures look fab, and you are delighted because you have happy clients. Tim Hardy is referable.

Paul Webster, I like to refer to him as my bank manager. Paul works for the bank I am with, although does the bank manager role still exist? Paul Webster is referable. I met Paul in the very early days of setting up a business. Back then another bank looked after my account. Paul was funny, and kind and hosted a business event for SMEs locally. He asked for help, could I host it, do a workshop, a speech, or some fun training? "Yes please!" It was the beginning of a friendship. A year or so later, I switched accounts, not because of a rate deal or special offer, but because of Paul. He continues to look out for opportunities for me and I continue to refer him. One time somehow, during a workshop his bank, the CEO, (the big gun if you like) joined. I have pictures of him joining in. The CEO was happy, Paul was happy and so was I. Over the years referring SMEs, manufacturing companies and, big organisations to Paul is easy. He is referable, the bank is good, logo nice, but it is all about liking and trusting Paul.

Referring someone can go wrong, wrong. Often in networking groups, there can be an expectation that to be there next week you must refer this week. There are many forms of networking (which we look at in the next chapter) and for some this commitment to share referral weekly works.

Referring this way is not my cup of tea, although I am always looking for an opportunity to help others in my network and when it naturally arises doing so, with an email and detail - this is a referral after all not, a lead. Paying it forward tends to come back at you, often when least expected. Receiving a thank-you for a referral is also a nice touch.

The time it went wrong. I was attending a networking group that looked for you to pass referrals, it was on the agenda, so had to happen. There was a recruitment chap, he came across well, nice, friendly, and keen to work in more businesses locally. It is worth noting that I'd only met this chap at networking on a handful of occasions. With hindsight, a few 121s, coffees, or at least digging deeper would have been a good idea.

My colleague for many years was John. A well-known and reputable businessman with a portfolio of companies. John's focus was on a new entrepreneurial idea, and it was taking off, he needed support. He wanted someone to find a business opportunity and be proficient with the office systems so everything could be logged. Usually, he would put an advert in the paper but that seemed old hat now, John was old school and the last advert bombed. I mentioned this as a referral to the recruiter at the next meeting and breathed a sigh of relief that this time I was not the one sitting and squirming with embarrassment at not helping the rest of the group.

The referral was backed up in writing, introducing the recruiter to John, followed by the detail, and suggesting that they meet. The good news, they did meet, and the recruiter found John a new employee. John was happy, job done - nearly. The recruiter was happy, £8,000 placement fee in his bank account.

The happiness was short-lived. The new employee was less than qualified, her system knowledge was nil, and she was struggling even to turn on the PC. Patiently, John and others helped. After a month no new business opportunity had been created and worse still it transpired, she had been waitressing and making puddings in her last job. That was missing from the CV. A younger member of the team made a comment about how she dressed, which could be seen as unprofessional. Next, she was off ill, felt humiliated, embarrassed by the comment, and said John made it. A week later a legal letter claiming that she had been treated unfairly and she wanted special conditions if she was to return or a £25,000 payout. The letter happened to mention her links with the local paper.

John could not believe what was happening. He just wanted to do business. He went back to the recruiter for clarity, reassurance and absolutely a refund. The recruiter said no, avoided John's call and ignored all correspondence.

John was furious. It later transpired the lady had done this several times to other employers in the county and received substantial payouts. Oddly, this was omitted from her bogus CV or made-up references. John had been played. The recruiter was ignoring him and that left me.

We still speak, occasionally. The lesson is obvious. Knowing, liking, and trusting take time. If you're going to refer someone, do it knowing everything about them and not just because it is on an agenda. It can go wrong, very wrong.

Thank you, such a small word that can win you even more referrals. When you are referred say thank you to the person who referred you.
Toby looks up "Come on Sally, this is common sense?"

Toby is correct, it is common sense and yet it is often ignored. The excitement of receiving a quality referral is big but forgetting to say thank you is a bad idea. I have sent bottles of gin, thank you cards, chocolate, and champagne. I have received flowers, chocolates, champagne, and gin. It's not about the gift, size, or value it is about the thank-you. Saying a heartfelt thank you to the wonderful person in your network who has sold you. When you omit to say thank you, it is unlikely you will be referred again any time soon. Say thank you however and the kindness you have been shown this time will be replicated. It is just good manners and good business.

When thanked by a company I have referred, using social media to again pay it forward is easy. A picture of the chocolates, a post about how you received a gift from said company and how lovely they are. With limited knowledge of algorithms, I do know that a picture of chocolate or cake can generate thousands of views! Positive PR for the company that you referred.

Referrals are your fastest route to a sale if you constantly ask in the right way and at the right time. To receive referrals your customer experience needs to be sensational. Get this part of the mix right and business will follow.

15 Networking

Networking is a magnificent tool in the prospecting toolbox!

Networking is about who knows you and what you provide. You get to know people, their companies and what they provide. You create rapport, build connections, and create a referral culture. Networking is an opportunity to meet with people and build trusting relationships. Sunny loved networking and after a year or two recognised the benefits, quality introductions and valued relationships.

Sensational Sunny always created a professional first impression! He viewed networking as an opportunity to meet and build trusting relationships. He was interested in the new people he met and wanted to learn about them. Sunny found reasons to connect and stay connected, nurture, and follow up. He let people know what he could do for them, not what he does, by sharing stories of successful sundial projects. Sunny was precise about his ideal referral and always followed up.

Sunny's polar opposite is Tim or Talkative Tim as he was known. Tim created a terrible first impression! He was disinterested in new people that he met and much preferred to talk at volume, about himself. Tim's conversation was always about him. He ignored any reason to connect, nurture and follow up. He shared boring details all about himself and his company and talked way longer than the allocated time. Tim would interrupt others' conversations to share his prices, catalogue, route plan and components and then he kept talking about himself. Tim viewed networking as an opportunity to sell special offers and talk at people.

Tim could not figure out why people enjoyed networking, after a month he thought it a waste of time and money. Tim was a character; you might recognise him. Years ago, at a prestigious networking event, I found there were many characters. The story (with names changed of course) is below, it showcases networking no, no's - can you spot them?

"Up 'issen!"

Tarquin was definitely, to quote a northern phrase, "Up 'issen"! (Translation - up himself!)

Tarquin, 6ft tall, was wearing red trousers and a tweed jacket and stood in the room, masterfully displaying the power pose, hands on hips and prepared to strut. Clenching a large, glossy brochure, Tarquin was on a mission.

We were both at a brilliant, very busy networking event. The coffee was fabulous, the breakfast delicious and the opportunities to meet new people were superb.

Tarquin, clearly less used to networking, was going about it all wrong. He had been engaged in conversation with Mike for a long time, so, politely, I joined in with their conversation. Networking etiquette - a smile and a "May I?" and off we go. Tarquin had a very long job title, which clearly delighted him but meant little to anyone else. Twice he announced his title and even then, I needed clarification as to what he did and who he was looking to meet. Next came his huge faux pas! Tarquin was only looking to meet one specific, very, very high-end contact. Those were his words! At that moment, glossy brochure in hand, Tarquin dismissed everyone else in the room as being of no consequence to him. Strangely, he did not seem to consider that anyone else could possibly lead him to his target client. As short-sighted goes, Tarquin was the perfect example.

Mike, the other gentleman, 55 and in a grey suit, was something to do with tax, which, by his admission, is often a conversation killer. I asked Mike who he was looking to gain an introduction to and was pleased to lead him across to some key people. Paying forward, connecting people, instigating relationships, and planting seeds, make networking gatherings a powerful place to create those vital referrals we are all looking out for.

I looked back across the room and there was Tarquin, chest puffed out, on his own! Out on a limb!

Further along, Amy, 28 and Annabel, 25 were sitting. I know – *sitting*! If ever there was a rule book for how not to network, sitting down would be in the top 5! From a law firm and evidently a little nervous, the ladies had found vacant chairs and were owning them. However, being seated meant that anyone approaching them, regardless of height, would tower above them. It's just not conducive to easy introductions, conversations and relationship building, is it? Amy and Annabel needed to stand up, park the nerves and mingle.

Stella, 52, an experienced networker, was mingling beautifully, chatting, including others, and introducing them easily. She was good right up to the point when she proffered a business card. I could see it was worn, with ink scribbled over the name of whoever the card had previously belonged to. Oh, so bad! Such a poor impression of her company! Why didn't Stella's boss splash the cash and show his respect for her and her contacts by keeping her supplied with pristine business cards?

Worse still was Boris. Boris was a well-known and most likeable gentleman of a certain age who thought everyone knew him and so did not need to bring any business cards. Pop that in the top five mistakes as well, a huge display of pompous arrogance, assuming people know who you are. He had forgotten the benefits of new business relationships and potential referrals. Bad job, Boris! Schoolboy error? The line between confidence and arrogance has always been slim, but in business when networking, making new contacts and growing relationships it really matters. I suggest that a slice of humility should be added to the mix. Humility, kindness and paying forward work. Funny how easy it is to scupper opportunities for building profitable long-term business relationships!

I spotted Tarquin towards the end of the event, rushing to try and catch a word with his target client as they were walking off to their next meeting. As it happens, I know the person well, as did others in the Networking Group. Any of us could have led Tarquin, with his fancy job title and glossy brochure, straight to the person he was after, much earlier on. It's like I said if Tarquin were less "Up 'issen", he would be way more successful.......

Networking is a superb way to meet your ideal prospect if you do it right. Investing time with ideal prospects, and proactively getting to know and support the group. Following up with coffee, understanding how you can help them. Avoid being a Today Only Tony, handing out a flyer or talking at people with a one-day-only special offer.

11 Visual Tips to Becoming a brilliant networker:

Tip 1, the picture is of a love heart. Love what you do! It's a given and common sense but remains number one, being excited about your product or service, and being proud to advertise your company will radiate. Be that person who lights up a room, not necessarily all showy and loud but confident, happy, and believing in who you are, why you are there and what you do. If struggling to understand this, the opposite would be a Sighing Sandra always moaning, looking miserable ready to blame pretty much anyone and everyone about most things. Radiate positivity (ch2) and people will all want to be around you, useful in a networking scenario.

Tip 2 shows a picture of big power station chimneys. They represent being a power source of information. Being a power source of information for others is invaluable. For example, if you meet Tom Lawrence, an estate agent at a networking event, he will happily share information on an accountant, offer to introduce you to a web designer or, suggest you meet a local solicitor who is very good. Tom spends his time paying it forward, being a power source of information for those in his network. Over many years Tom has used this method, being sincere in thinking about whom he can introduce and to whom. Tom is kind, well received and frequently referred. Paying it forward and creating a referral culture is a fab idea when it feels correct as opposed to because you are asked to leave a group if you don't.

Tip 3 - a question mark. As mentioned in the sales process, ask questions. Not just any questions! Ask true, open questions.
In networking, one brilliant way to encourage conversation is by beginning with "Tell me..." or "Share with me..."

When networking, firing questions at a stranger will turn them off. "What do you do?" Swiftly followed by, "Why do you do that?" Then quickly into "Where do you do that?" Then, "How do you do that?" Next, "When did that begin?" and "Why that way?" "Who else do you work with?" This feels rude and more like an interrogation.

True open questions are reserved for networking with strangers and are a fast-track way to build rapport. Begin with "Tell me about yourself, share your plans with me." They are lovely soft, slippers of questions. True, open questions can see strangers really open up about themselves at networking. If they talk about themselves and you listen without 'but', (ch 8) their limbic brain thinks you are nice. Win!

Tip 4 - the picture is of a football reaching the back of the net - goal! So, what is yours? Most activities in business require a measure of return on investment, ROI. In networking, this means a return on your time and money. Remember, networking is not selling, although measuring the success of an event is necessary if you want to avoid wasted time.

What is your goal and have you written it down? If going for the first time to a new group with approximately 30 members, your goal might be to connect with 20, follow up with 10 and book meetings with 2. The numbers will reflect the type of group and how long you have been going. Importantly, have a goal and share it. Savvy salespeople note in their CRM where they met new prospects, and this enables analysis 12 months later as to which group works best.

Remember, networking is a tool in the toolbox, and understanding which brand of this tool delivers the best return (time and money) is a good idea.

Tip 5, (Picture of LinkedIn logo) LinkedIn, or other social media. Connecting on LinkedIn post networking is a brilliant idea. It allows you to send a personalised message and connect. Suddenly, although only a flicker, you now have a connection to someone who could one day become a client. Way off a sale or even a coffee this connection is a beginning. Not connecting on LinkedIn when a prospect has met you, maybe heard how you help others who look just like they do, is a missed opportunity. Being able to view and learn more about your project is a good way to continue to nurture this relationship.

As well as LinkedIn, if you meet someone whom you click with, who could be an ideal prospect or if you are keen to make a great impression you could bring out - the car park email. When you get back to the car, send a message from your phone. "Really good to meet today. Your comment about blue elephants was on point. Let's stay in touch. Best wishes." Be standout and memorable for the right reasons.

It's short, sweet and stands out. Send a car park email backed up with a LinkedIn connection with a message and the next time you call, your chances of being put through are soaring!

Tip 6 (Picture of rabbit with very big ears) Listen without "but". This could be a good time to re-read the chapter "Say Less, Sell More" all about the importance of active listening. So very true and necessary when networking. Sunny was brilliant at listening and in particular noting and highlighting the reason why a follow-up call/meeting could be a good idea. Sunny was listening out for buying signals. Being sincerely interested, not looking across a shoulder to the back of the room or checking emails if networking virtually. People know what you are doing, and it is just rude. Listen intently to the person who is talking, and you will be amazed by what you can learn. We were blessed with two ears and one mouth for good reason.

Tip 7 Be clear - eat later. (Picture of an egg sandwich) Have you tried balancing an egg and cress sandwich, sausage roll, hummus, carrot sticks, and oven-baked crisps on a paper plate, whilst standing shoulder to shoulder in a busy hotel meeting room? Add in a cup on a saucer, a bag on a shoulder and a speaker on a mission to get through the crowd, all this while you are supposed to be networking? How to balance food, swerve around people and enjoy engaging in conversation when your mouth is full! The cup goes flying, the carrot stick launches across the room, and you hang on to the saucer.

As we are talking about saucers, why do they exist? Really why do hotels feel the need to provide a tiny cup on a saucer? Bring on the mugs, big, sturdy mugs, one drink required, fewer trips to refill and less washing up. Potentially lose the saucer and save the planet. Maybe not that simple but if you are a hotelier reading this, please take note.

Back to eating. Do it later, eat before you network, eat while sitting down and the speaker is on, and eat afterwards - just do not sabotage the precious time with ideal prospects to dance with a sandwich and speak with a mouth full.

Be clear, speak well and remember to smile.

Tip 8. Let's chat. But what to chat about? It is a common question and easy common points of interest are a good idea. Avoiding politics, the weather, religion, and the journey is a good idea. Staying on positive, relatable topics is way safer. Tell me about your holidays. Share about your Christmas plans. Tell me about the weekend, the new house, or car. A winning question. Where are you from? Is comfortable and will see the person you're asking reply with a geographical place or a business.

"Tell me…" or "Share with me…" are True Open Questions and a great way to begin a conversation. One time a lady stopped to ask, "What if they start telling me everything?" If they tell me about their divorce, office mole, or the secret code to something, then what?" When asking a true open question about a CPI (Common Point of Interest) you will only be told about what people are happy to share.

Tip 9. Look the part and wear a name badge. OK, so a huge lanyard might not go with your carefully chosen outfit. Putting a badge on that is made of anything but bling may not be on trend or adhere to your brand guidelines, but you need to wear your badge. People need to know who you are, and a badge helps. When looking at names please try and avoid the prolonged stare - it can look odd especially if looking straight at a lady's cleavage. Just saying!

As well as a name badge, what you choose to wear for networking matters if you want to create a great first impression. You might think that being judged only on what you do or say is important, that nothing else should matter, especially appearance. The slight flaw is that we are human beings, wired to form an opinion about someone based on how they look. It's just how it is! It is the reason conmen dress like people in authority to dupe, fool and con. If you dress like you're a gardener and turn up to a professional networking event in muddy wellies, scruffy jeans and a worn jumper people will assume you are a busy gardener. Dressing to impress not only boosts self-confidence but also showcases you and your business in the right or wrong way. This is covered in A Fabulous First Impression (chapter 7) and is worthy of a repeat. Dress well and people will, in a matter of seconds create a positive impression of you before you say a word.

In your pocket, bag, or folder please have a business card or two. Covid made us all think twice about sharing a business card, could it be dangerous, should we throw them all away? My suggestion would be to take your business cards, offer or if requested hand them over. It is another great way to be remembered after the event. Otherwise, phone apps and QR codes are a good idea, but there is something rather lovely about sharing a business card, if it's a good one that is.

Tip 10 Be You! I know this should be common sense, but it is often forgotten. People quiver at the thought of sharing space with strangers and melt into a way smaller version of themselves. Others think because they have been in post at a very smart law firm, that by default they are far too important to talk to strangers, hang their own coat or take business cards. The Tarquin story summarises this beautifully.

Simply be you. With all your wonderfulness and the unique personality that you bring to networking. Trying to be anyone but you is pointless and you will be found out. If it's your first time that is OK, everyone has a first time. If you're terrified then be brave, it won't be that bad, I promise. Being authentic is a brilliant quality in wonderful salespeople. Will everybody like you? Probably not, it's a life thing. You don't need everyone to like you, just to be in an environment with other like-minded businesspeople and prospects. Being liked by everyone won't happen, stop overthinking and just be you.

Tip 11 Repeat, repeat, repeat! Going to networking once with the expectation that the sales will follow a single meeting is deluded. People do of course, like Today Only Tony. He would rush around with a flyer for everyone, trying to convince you to buy, meet or call, right away. Oh dear, a bad idea and a huge turnoff. Networking is not selling. Dropping flyers and being pushy are.

Remember, big fish go slow. This is the beginning of a relationship, not a one-night stand. It could take months, quarters, or years before you are trusted. Dig deep, invest time, and really understand the people who are in the room. Follow-up and just a coffee help enormously with this. When you have tried several, choose groups you enjoy, and which are most likely to deliver a return and get to know them. Sign up for everything, throw yourself in at full throttle and become familiar with and trusted in your group. So long as you're with the right people it will pay dividends.

Networking groups vary in format, style, and feel. Some are drinks at a bar without a clear agenda, and others are carefully structured right down to passing referrals. Often at breakfast, lunch, or tea, there will be a request for you to deliver sixty seconds, sometimes referred to as an elevator pitch. This is your moment to showcase what you do, who you have helped, the solutions delivered, and the opportunities created for your clients. Showcasing your offering in a third-party testimonial is a great idea. Instead, frequently this is what happens.

Networking story - Wing It Wayne heard his name being called. He was invited to give his sixty seconds; he was informed that a bell would go off if he overran. Wayne shuffled in his chair, wasting precious seconds. Nervously he pushed the chair back, stood up and looked at the others enjoying breakfast. He coughed and said, "Hi!" He thanked the group for being a group, mentioned how lovely the breakfast was, the eggs Benedict in particular, he commented on the room decor, saying it looked funky. Wayne fidgeted and then said he was in IT and did tech stuff and began to list each product and service, cloud, software, cyber - and then the bell went off. Relieved his time was up, Wayne sat down. He wasn't too bothered, no one had looked up when he was talking, but the breakfast really was delicious.

Frequently Wayne's sixty seconds is repeated in networking groups across the UK. An unprofessional dollop of waffle instead of relishing and maximising the opportunity to showcase what your business does, a free advert that if done well could see you talked about and remembered by the room full of people for years to come.

On-it-Olly was up next. He looked the part in his lilac suit and his voice commanded attention.

Harrogate Law firm held to ransom!

All eyes looked up, cutlery was put down, and Olly had the room's attention. Next, the name is spoken twice.

"Olly, On It Olly of A Super Tech Company."

Olly then shared the story of the law firm that looked just like the others in the room and how this law firm thought cyber-attack would never happen to them. He shared how they passed over tech audits and offers of cyber checks thinking they were too small, and they would be ok. Olly then shared how the cleaner unknowingly let cyber software into the system and weeks later everything halted. The law firm had to spend thousands trying to remedy the attack. The room was still hooked on Olly's words, listening to his relatable story, and nodded at the suggestion that they would have been better training all staff, that preventing and being proactive was a far better idea.

Olly asked for introductions to law firms and the IT directors by name. Pencils picked up and notes were made.

Olly repeated his name and how he helped companies.

No bell, he sat down and smiled as people went back to eating. Each week Olly shared a different story, all about how he helped businesses, be it cloud storage, cyber-security, or laptops, the topic always specific to the people around the table. His sixty seconds appeared to be off the cuff, but they had been written months ago and sat in a file ready to be pulled.

Olly's group knew how he helped companies and the results he achieved for them. Olly frequently received calls from people who had heard about him from the group. Networking for Olly was a win because he used his sixty seconds wisely.

Olly's focus was on networking and when tasked with delivering his sixty seconds he knew he needed to showcase how he helped companies. Early on, Olly followed these steps when crafting a catalogue of sixty-second presentations around key areas in which his potential clients 'needed help:

1. Headline - four maybe five words max. What could Olly say to stop the room from eating, sit up and pay attention to his story? It is a bold move, and many prefer to begin with their name, but if you want to be remembered, become familiar and build awareness, a strong headline is a great starting point.

2. Your name twice. Sally, Sally Roberts. In training, we go around the room doing this. It will sound odd to begin with and it needs practice to become a habit. It sounds a bit like James Bond, but why not? Again, to be remembered and become familiar, deliver your name twice. It works! Especially if new to a group with people you have never met, saying your name twice and then the company, is a good idea.

3. Next, relate a story created specifically for your audience. We all love a story, it's memorable'|. For sixty seconds though, use characters that share how they felt, the problem they had to face and how you and your company became the superheroes that solved it. Give details, and paint pictures to make it memorable. Go wild with the happy ending. The measure of a good story, will it be remembered hours after your breakfast meeting.

4. When given the opportunity to ask for a referral, be specific about whom you want to work with and ask for an introduction.

If you don't ask you won't get, it really is that simple. Caution - if you do as many do and ask to speak to every business in the county who might happen to need what you offer, I promise no one will write down any names. If, however, you have planned, checked who might know an ideal-looking prospect and asked for them by name, watch as your new colleagues write your preferred introduction down on paper. People are kind and want to help, if you have a name there is a greater chance someone will have a link.

Props are a good idea, showing a diamond ring is way more impactful than just talking. There was a prestige jeweller in a group I went to and every week a new piece of stunning jewellery would be passed around the room. He very quickly shared how wonderful his jewellery was, he very quickly had a new group of people advocating his work.

Before moving on from networking, hear a true story about a wonderful lady, Jenni Brown. She attended training on networking and creating a sixty-second pitch. Understanding that to be effective, sixty seconds had to be memorable and relevant to the room she created a magnificent elevator pitch. It began with the statement, "I sort people's piles!" Everyone looked up and chuckled we were hooked. Jenni was a freelance PA, and she did sort piles - of papers, data, and stuff. I forget the story in detail, it was good, but the headline was right up there as one of the best.

So, you have been networking, now what? Now for the follow-up. Refer to your goals (set pre-event). Who to connect to? Everyone or just some? Reach out and connect on LinkedIn with a personal message referencing where you met. If someone made an impression, then perhaps time for the car park email. Avoid waffle, be on it, and stand out for being different. You are building familiarity and awareness after all. Schedule a coffee, just a coffee (ch6) to learn about them and share about you. Just a coffee, not a sales call but a great way of nurturing relationships within a group. Lastly, go back and network some more. Sometimes nurturing big fish can take years, invest your time in getting to know, like and trust all the group members. Be proactive in booking 121s afterwards. Be at other networking groups and be on the radar of your prospects for all the right reasons.

How can you find out where to network? I call it Tug a Topic, ask Google, look at Eventbrite. Enter networking with your location, industry type, or sector. The results will surprise you. LinkedIn can help as well so long as your network is established, search for networking or ask your network for suggestions. Maybe # the sector or location to narrow down search results. Either way, get tugging and you will be rewarded.

Networking can be great fun! You will learn lots and meet plenty of new people in business with a similar perspective. The win in networking is that the next time you put in a "cold" call you will most likely get put through. The decision maker now knows who you are. You have met, had a coffee, are connected, and interact on LinkedIn. The toolbox needs all the tools used in conjunction with each other, and with consistency and commitment, it will generate sensational results.

When you learn to network well you become like a bridge. John Burgess is an accountant who I met years ago. He had attended training and we have stayed in touch. He networks well, in many places across the North, mostly Leeds. John Burgess is a well-known face and often meets for "Just Coffee" or calls for a catch-up. He posts on LinkedIn and is unquestionably a familiar, well-known face when it comes to accounting. I have referred him several times and he is front of mind when someone is talking about tax, accounts, or finance.

The LinkedIn post read "Being front of mind takes time. Meeting at networking events, lunches, and exhibitions. Knowing to follow up with coffee, a beer, or breakfast. Learning about the person, the business and how you can help them. Supporting on social media. Then when they need what you do, you are front of mind and receive the call. Being front of mind takes time and energy. John Burgess, you nailed it. Walking over a bridge yesterday and there was a sign. Who did I think of? #Frontofmind #nailedit #awarenessmatters

John replied, "It's also a long game, some of my best clients / referrals have taken years to come to fruition!"

To be successful at prospecting, be like John Burgess, and become a bridge.

16 The Sales Call

Just call! Cold warm or hot, just call!

Remember when all phones had dials, you put your finger in a numbered hole and went full circle before releasing only to repeat the process six times. You had to stay rooted in the same spot as the phone because it was plugged into the wall. Six digits and you would be ringing the person on the other end and if lucky, get connected. Area codes were needed on occasion, but they were costly. Using the phone was costly. Calling was often done after 6 pm at the off-peak rate as it was far too expensive during the day. Weekends were also off-peak and so cost less and families would plan to make calls on a Saturday or Sunday. Only emergency calls were made in peak times and there was a genuine worry that someone had died if you happened to receive a phone call in peak hours! Often, call duration was short, and even timed as parents of teenagers wanted their children to be off the phone. It costs money you know!

Interestingly, back then your phone number would be listed in a BT Phone book and all businesses featured in the Yellow Pages or Thompson Local telephone directory. If you were clever and not wanting to be found you could be taken off the list, but it was rare. Most people could be found in the phone book. Deliveries of Yellow Pages must have weighed a ton and taken ages to deliver. I recall a copy for each house stacked in huge piles on the road corner. Often, they were used as steps, a stool to help you reach a cupboard,

Today, just forty or so years later and the transformation in phone communication is staggering. Arguably teenagers are still glued to their phones, their own phones! Now we can call who we want, when we want, wherever we are for very little money, and we can call from the car. Our phones store numbers, record times and call duration. Numbers are now found via Google or other search engines and so phone books have quickly become a thing of the past.

The phone as a method of communication is brilliant. We have a lot to thank Alexander Graham Bell for. Other methods of communication have crept in, and some have taken over our need to call. We can use WhatsApp, Text, and Facebook messaging and yet the phone remains a key tool in the prospecting toolbox.

During the recent Covid pandemic, our call times went up. The good old-fashioned method of picking up the phone and talking to someone suddenly seemed like a fabulous idea, a more intimate means of communication.

So, if the phone is so very good, and is known for igniting the brain and getting a prospect or client's jelly wobbling, why oh why do we avoid it?

"Jelly?" asks Toby.

 - The brain Toby. Your brain is like a big lump of jelly, and your job in sales, if you want to sell more, is to make your prospects' jelly wobble. If you text, email or write to a prospect, rarely does the jelly wobble. If you call, Zoom, or better still meet face to face, brilliant, the jelly begins to wobble. When jelly wobbles sales soar, making a call is a great way to get the jelly wobbling.

Nobody answers a phone that does not ring, so why such a lack of dialling? If you want to succeed in sales, start interrupting! Interrupt your prospect's day to talk about something you want them to hear, do or buy. It's not about cold, warm, or hot, it's about picking up the phone.

To reduce fear of cold calling you could do Cold Calling Courses, watch YouTube, and learn tips, tricks and incredible opening lines that promise to turn you into a cold calling ninja! Oh, dear! Please pause, avoid trying to be someone else, pick up the phone and just be you.

Do you recognise the salesperson who, when about to dial, becomes somebody else, a smarmier, slightly greasy salesperson? They lean back in their chair, hands behind their head and smile into the headset microphone. Then it goes like this: -
"Hi, Ethel, today is your lucky day because you are talking to me!" The call is cut off.

Next try: -
"Hi, I'm not trying to sell you anything…" Gone!

Next: -
"This is HMRC and I want to speak with your …" Gone!

The most common one is this: -
"Hello! This is (name here) and I am a salesperson from a company trying to sell you something." Blocked!

There are so many awful examples of salespeople with scripts, tricks and super slick ways that simply see a call halted and worse still, give salespeople a bad name.

Before looking at cold calls in detail, any call is to a human being, a person with a brain, in particular a limbic part of the brain. In a few seconds, they decide whether they like and trust you. If your opening gambit was, I am here to sell to you, in a smarmy voice, are you at all surprised they hung up? In business, many companies block calls as we can block numbers on our mobile phones. To stand out you could try being human, being real, being you!

Let's talk about the gatekeeper. In training, this is usually where the murmuring and groans begin. As expected, Toby's hand is up.

"Sally, the gatekeeper is awful, a cow, evil, the whole purpose of the gatekeeper is to prevent me from being put through to the decision maker." Toby is still going, clearly with a point to make. "I'm convinced the gatekeeper wakes up every day and plans to destroy my activity sales target!"

- Wow, Toby you really don't like the gatekeeper, and just a hunch, I am guessing you rarely get through to any decision-makers.

"Never Sally, that is why I hate them so much."

Time for a re-frame Toby. Time to see Ethel through a different lens.

"Ethel?" asks Toby.
- Yes, Ethel!

Do you view the gatekeeper as trouble, annoying or put on earth to ensure you never get to talk to the decision maker? Time for a shift in mindset! Ethel is delightful, a grandma in fact. Working with Steve & Co for many years she is known for doing a good job. Her boss trusts, likes and respects her. Ethel receives many prospecting calls, some good, some bad, some downright awful. Ethel understands the callers have a job to do but expects good manners and courtesy. Sometimes, if it feels right, she puts the caller through.

There are seven common sense suggestions to see you build a connection with Ethel and in time see you put through. A very big warning! It takes time, you might get lucky and be put through straight away. Great! However, in the interest of managing the expectation, it usually takes between 3 and 8 times before this happens. Bring out polite persistence. Please don't give up and write this off as nonsense after one attempt.

The first suggestion is to be likeable. In previous chapters, I have mentioned the importance of being liked. Connect with Ethel, build rapport, talk geography, mention the company, tell a joke or whatever it takes to make Ethel smile and you liked. This works best when you are being real. Try asking for help. Toby has his head in his hands.

"So, you want me to reframe my view of Ethel and then ask her for help? Like that is going to work?"

Toby's comment is expected and common. I share the story of Chris, new in a sales role in radio advertising. We were on our way back from Skipton and Chris was sharing his less-than-successful track record of being put through to a new prospect. He explained that he was targeting dentists for a new show that required sponsorship. He knew it could be a great opportunity but so far had been unable to share just how great, as the gatekeeper was a determined blocker. I asked what his call was like and true to form he called up, bypassed any rapport, and asked to speak to the dentist. Dr Wong, Chris was informed, was busy. Chris then gave up. He tried a few days later and gave up again as Dr Wong was still busy. Chris believed this prospect was a no-go and that it was impossible to speak with him.

Recognising Chris's frustration and keen to share how it could look with a few tweaks, I called the Dental Practice from the car on speaker.

Ethel answered a standard reception answer. The call looked a little like this: -

"Hello, you're through to The Dental Practice, how may I help you?"

"Hello, thank you for a speedy pick-up, and yes, I do hope you can help me. Sorry, what was your name, please?"

"It's Ethel."

"Good morning, Ethel, I am just driving back from Skipton, a stunning autumnal morning. What is it like in Harrogate today?"

Ethel began to reply, sharing about the leaves, the change in season and how it would be Christmas soon, that the council had begun putting up the lights. Ethel informed us that it was dry now and quite mild for the time of year.

I listened and added in an occasional umm and ahh to prove I was listening. Then I asked,

"Ethel, you kindly offered to help, would that still be ok?"

"Yes, of course, at least I will try," replied Ethel.

I explained that the local radio station had a documentary-style show about dental hygiene and really, we wanted to speak to Dr Wong as he was a trusted dentist in the region. To date getting to speak to him had been tricky and I wondered what was the best thing to do.

Ethel agreed he was a busy dentist and then she suggested we meet him and booked a face-to-face visit after his surgery on Thursday.

Ethel left the call smiling and feeling good. She had been helpful and enjoyed a pleasant chat. I was happy as showcasing the importance of being real and asking for what you want politely delivered a meeting. Chris was stunned!

This is probably not accurate word for word as it was years ago but the important lesson to learn is building rapport, being real and asking for what you want. The Culture Code book by Daniel Coyle shares the rainy-day experiment at the station. A stranger wanting to borrow a phone approached another stranger on the platform. When taking time to build rapport by talking about the weather before requesting to borrow a phone there was a 422% increase in "Yes". Omit to build rapport at your peril it can increase positive outcomes exponentially!

Other suggestions for improving your chances of Ethel putting you through to the decision-maker are as follows.

1. Be likeable

2. Be polite, use please and good manners
3. Be honest - who are you and where from
4. Connect with Ethel - build rapport
5. Hold the tricks, don't pretend to be from HMRC
6. Ask for help
7. If super keen, call before Ethel arrives or goes home

Cold calling takes persistence, it is noted that it takes an average of 8 calls before you will get put through to the decision maker. The good news is that if you do get put through there is a strong chance, he or she wants to buy from you. So, make it count!

Before showing you a proven rather fabulous call method here is a tip to reduce the number of times you need to call.

If using all the tools in the toolbox and prospecting or fishing in ponds where your ideal big fish are, then you should be getting known. LinkedIn, networking exhibitions, referrals, just coffee, mixing and using all the tools will build familiarity and awareness of you and the solutions you bring. If the prospect has heard your name, seen your posts talking about how you delivered a solution for people just like him, walked past your exhibition stand or read your article, all these things combined will dramatically reduce the number of calls you need to make to be put through. Warning, please remember there is no magic trick or one method that will see you put straight through - persistence is still required. Ignoring all the other tools just to cold call day in and day out is possible but a real slog.

Some leaders, usually old school, and fans of cold calling, still request significant call activity day in and day out. Cold calling absolutely has a place and is effective as a part of the mix. When witnessing sales roles that are just cold calling, the churn is often high. New leaders see the value in passing autonomy to the salesperson. They know the target, make it about quality, face-to-face meetings, and then send them out to achieve. Using all the tools in the toolbox is a speedier route to face-to-face visits and overall sales success.

Back to the call. With Ethel, rapport was important. With a big fish, rapport still matters but if you are through, you need to make it count. The decision-maker's most precious commodity is time. So, go for it! Using the three steps, IBS, RBS, and Request to make an impression, deliver a positive message and book a visit.

Step1.
In training, I ask does anyone know what an IBS is. Usually, there are blank looks all around and on one occasion far too much info from a lady who did have IBS. Your IBS is your Introductory Benefit Statement. You introduce yourself, name twice and the benefit you bring.

an example:

IBS. **Hello. Matthew Lewis**, this is Rob, Rob Singh, The Technology Group. I keep engineering companies happy by ensuring their IT is protected from cyber-attack, is efficient and enables them to delight clients.

Step 2.
The RBS is the punchy part so make it relevant and count. Share the reason you're calling and the benefit. Tell a story about how you helped a company that had a big problem, most likely a problem that your decision-maker is all too familiar with. Then share how your company solved it, keeping it brief and impactful, with a happy ending, the transformation, results achieved and how they now refer you. Be passionate and confident and let your enthusiasm be infectious. When this call is over, will your RBS be remembered for all the right reasons?

Think testimonials, talk about results, and be confident and enthused.

RBS - I was recently working with a newly appointed MD at a large Yorkshire engineering company. He was struggling to find expert support and reassurance that his IT systems were safe from attack and supporting engineers who operated remotely across the UK. He invited our expert team in to analyse what was needed and make suggestions. He understood us, liked us, and chose to bring us in as partners with his IT team. The team now work remotely with ease and dials into all meetings, engineers can be tracked, and the time saving has been immense. He is so happy he now refers The Technology Company and sleeps soundly knowing all systems are safe.

Step 3, is the request.
Time to ask for what you want - a face-to-face visit.

Toby is looking at you! "Surely after that RBS, you would just ask if they wanted to meet?" Toby is correct, however, understanding the language used within a request can tip a "maybe" over to a "yes".

Your request to meet needs to assume they will want to. Having just heard an incredible testimonial why wouldn't they? Your belief that you can help needs to radiate. Caution, remember this is a first call and being too salesy could be a big turn-off. No one likes to be sold to, so it's time to pull it back. Include in your request that a visit is to ascertain if you might be a fit, might be their cup of tea, and could offer a solution, just a little U-turn on a very powerful request.

Simply, you are trying to keep the prospects system one brain saying yes and the language you use at this step can influence their decisions.

Instead of, "We should meet because I know I can help protect your IT," try this!

Request: "I believe The Tech Company could benefit your

organisational sites and engineers. Would you like to meet, or book a visit so I can learn about your requirements and see if we might be a fit? **Would it be OK if** we schedule a call next week for Thursday or Friday?" and sshhh!

The request displays belief but is softer, and easier to agree with and the keyword "believe", usually saved for religion, displays real confidence. You don't just think you might be able to help, your thoughts are not grey or murky they are definite and specific. Using "could" instead of "should" keeps their system one brain calm, you're not telling the decision maker what to do. No one wants to be told what to do, so provide autonomy. If you want to learn about their business, you might have fifty years or more IT experience but suggesting to a decision-maker that their business is unique is a nice touch. Might be a fit, a pullback again so system one brain remains calm. You're not saying you are a fit, the power is back with the decision maker. "Would it be OK if..." and pause is a great way to receive a yes before they know what they are saying yes to, then a choice of days for a call or visit.

The cold call following this process will take time to perfect -but it does work. One of the very first companies I trained logged everything, from calls to appointments being a key performance indicator. After using this technique, the call-to-visit ratio soared.

Nurture Ethel, build rapport and when through to the decision maker make it count. Standout for delivering a powerful testimonial and be liked for the language you use. Your "Yes" rate will increase - it's just what happens!

17 Voicemail

Say nothing and miss out!

When you call a prospect or a client, how often do you get through to an answer phone, voicemail or diverted to the main office?

Faced with two options, hang up or leave a voicemail what do you do?

In training the headline is simple, no hook no callback.

Toby squirms and then says, "Sally it is so cringe leaving a voicemail, what do you say? Usually, I get all flustered or sometimes carry on and leave a huge message that sees me being cut off mid-flow."

Many do just as Toby does. They avoid leaving a voicemail for fear of sounding odd or worse still they fill the voicemail and talk for many minutes thinking that will help call duration.

It is easy when you call out and receive an answer phone, leave a message that follows a format. If you simply hang up, then that day you and your company are not on the prospect's radar. Your voicemail can contribute to building familiarity and awareness of you.

Prospects & customers listen to voicemail so leave one. Better still if you include a hook, your callbacks can double! Try this format.

1. Hello Matthew, this is Olly, On it Olly.

2. 0123 456789, 0123 456789 slowly

3. Reason for the call, I noted your commennt o our LinkedIn

post about cyber-attacks and cloud storage.

4. Give a reason to call you - hook /curiosity "Last week The Tech Company launched a revolutionary cyber security package that is transforming remote working for engineers and most managing directors are thrilled. Would it be ok to call me back today please, as I believe this leading innovation could be of interest? Olly On It Olly, 0123 456789, 0123 456789", twice.

Always use your name twice, especially on the phone as there is no name badge to refer to. Picking up a call, those first few seconds can be lost, so repeating the name twice is a good idea.

Next state your phone number slowly and twice so it can be written down. If they want to speak to you excellent, they will call without listening to your hook.

Have a reason you are calling, not just "I am calling because I want to sell you something," find a credible, relatable reason.

Then the hook, like the RBS in a cold call needs punch, to be relevant and remembered. Sharing a testimonial from another MD who looks just like them will see the prospect take note. If they call, fab, if they don't you have successfully showcased how you help others who look just like them and how the results were outstanding. Your hook might see a callback today, it might see a callback next week. Make it count and remember, big fish go slow.

Lastly, ask for what you want politely, please call back today, add in a sprinkle of scarcity, repeat your number and wait for the phone to ring.

18 Email

Email if you must.

Companies teach us how to spot dodgy-looking emails, how never to open them, to delete them immediately and preferably report them. Emails from strangers hit firewalls, spam filters and default to junk on a good day.

Why then is there such an over-reliance on prospecting emails? Maybe because the fear of picking up the phone and having a conversation has enabled email to be viewed as a saviour. "Look, I can send 5 million emails at the press of a button at an automated time, all to people in a specific area. Yippee and how clever is that?" How awful! Sometimes a salesperson will meet a prospect or contact, add them to the CRM and tick yes to all marketing. A massive turn-off, someone you have met once is suddenly receiving email after email offering this deal, that deal or a new offer. Without intention, the salesperson encourages the potential prospect to turn them off and say no to future communication. Oh, dear!

I will share how to create a prospecting email; it is after all a part of the prospecting toolbox. Many companies might have you believe it is critical, but in business-to-business with a big fish, it will most likely be ignored. If more transactional and purchasing from you is a smaller, maybe impulse-driven decision, for example, a Black Friday offer on flowers, go wild, that is more likely to work.

Did you know that about 62% of emails are ignored, missed, and remain unopened? If not opened within 24 hours, then the chance of it ever being opened is slim to none. If you are going to email, make it count, stand out for the right reasons, and talk in the customer's or prospect's language about them.

In the summer I took a call from a successful MD who had been blind copied into an email from one of his established account managers. It was to an existing, valued customer and the shocking part is that it was all about the account manager. Each line included, "We do.", "I am..", "Our people.."., "The company.." Oh no, oh dear, a training need right there!

Fred's Fantastic Fridges was created soon after to showcase how not to email your clients. It is below, enjoy and try counting how many times the word me, *I, Fred, Fred's Fantastic Fridges or my* is used.

Hello Fiona!

Fred here from Fred's Fantastic Fridges. I am emailing to tell you how I have been looking at your account with Fred's Fantastic Fridges which is managed by me. I look after your account, and I personally plan to look after it well as I can.

Last week I noticed that our new range of ice cube shelves was not included in the delivery. I'm so upset by this that I thought I would sit on my new chair in my new white fridge-style office, and I would immediately write you an email from me, Fred.

I am so glad I can write this as I feel it is such a shame that I only spotted that it was missing yesterday. It is a good job that I look after your account, and you are being looked after by me.

I wondered if you'd like to go out for dinner with me, a customer treat from me and on me. I will put it on my expenses, so go wild. I get on well with the Finance Director so I am sure she will be happy to sign off my receipt. Where shall we go? I love the new Chinese on Station Parade, near my house and my Mum's house. I went last week with my friends, and I had the spring rolls, in fact, I ate six! I was full up! I thought they were delicious, and my friends had them as well. The restaurant staff were pleased I was there, and said I added a bit of "Je ne sais quoi". I did French GCSE; thought you'd like to know that about me. Let me know when suits you and I will sort it. You know me - I sort things.

Maybe I could do the karaoke sing-along again. I am very good. My mother taught me to sing when I was four. I was very cute - my family said so although my teacher was less polite. Would you like a picture of me, I am very popular and handsome.

Best wishes from me, Fred.
I look after your account at Fred's Fantastic Fridges.

Fred - call me on 01132 456789
Or on my special Fred mobile 07546 678901

Fred From Fred's Fantastic Fridges
Co-founder - see more about me, Fred, on my LinkedIn.

Five is the magic number, if your email to a client or a prospect has more than 5 of, *we, me, I, Our people, company name,* then it's time to rewrite. The most important person in your client's or prospect's life is them, so talk about them and receive greater buy-in and a chance that it will be read.

In training, people laugh at this example as one person reads the story. It is an idea to reread your emails to clients and consciously check that you are sticking to just 5.

You're looking to catch the attention of the prospect and the best way is to talk about them. Your cold call included a testimonial about a business that looked just like them. Your voicemail offered a hook that related to them, and your sixty seconds was a story with a happy ending about how you helped a company that looked like your prospect. For email to work, it needs to engage your prospect in the same way.

First, think about who the email is going to and make it specific to them. If you are just throwing a generic email out to as many people as possible, it is unlikely that your big fish will pay attention. However, spend time creating a short, five-word, snappy headline that immediately relates to your prospect and the chances are improved. If the headline is anything but powerful, your email will be ignored. Remember how easy it is to send emails to junk or delete, however great the deal is. If this is a first email, make it count, make it personal to them.

A suggestion to help improve the odds of your email arriving would be to remove the huge attachments, key spam words, video links and stacks of photos. They will most likely be blocked.

Of course, if you have met before there is a greater chance your email might be opened. An excellent start. Now is not the time to launch with a "Today Only Tony" special offer unless you want to undo the fabulous first impression you made at networking.

Your headline is snappy and about them, the prospect opens your email - and now what? You want them to continue reading and the most appealing topic you could mention is them. Specifically, the problems they might be having or opportunities they might want to create. It would be rude to launch right in with an assumption that you know for a fact that this is what they want, no one likes being told what to do. Take a step back and talk about the sector, industry, or profession and how it is experiencing problems and looking for opportunities. Show empathy and compliment the forward-thinking organisations who are looking for solutions. Above all, having demonstrated your understanding of the problems they might face, remember to be you, to be authentic and credible. Now is not the time for a special offer, a detailed pitch, or a spec sheet. Remember, Big Fish go slow.

The email is open, the decision-maker is reading it and nodding in agreement. They can relate to what you say. The email is spot on. Next, link to your company and how it solves problems and creates opportunities for the prospect. This is your moment, the time to pull the key, testimonial style, and relevant sentences. Add in a few powerful differentiators and know that by the end of the paragraph, your prospect will have new knowledge. They will now know you can help to take their problems away and create opportunities for them. Make it count!

Remember the cold call, the request when you use the word believe followed by a pullback such as, "See if we might be a fit for you?" The final part of the email is similar. Be clear about what you want (whether a call or meeting) and ask for it. As you might have heard before, it is how you ask that matters.

Launching right in with, "Shall we meet, because I know I am brilliant?" will most likely see you deleted. Such a shame after a good start. Pull back because, until you meet you are unsure if you can help. Say "I'm unsure if we might be a fit so shall we book a short call?" Make it easy for the prospect to say yes to the next step.

Manufacturer Protected from £8 million Cyber Attack!

Hello, Mr. IT Prospect!

Forward-thinking manufacturing companies understand the importance of protecting their IT systems. An increase in remote working, engineers off-site and temporary staff using the company Wi-Fi has led IT directors to recognise that they need to protect all infrastructure from attack. Knowing where to turn has proved tricky. Most companies are looking to combine security with IT support, software expertise, CRM, and cloud storage. Loading Norton onto a PC is no longer a solution and server storage is becoming unpopular. Where should you turn for quality, trusted expertise and support?

At A Technology Company, quality IT support and safety is our speciality. Listening to IT Directors and ensuring they are correctly guided and protected from attack is our niche. Our teams are all accredited, Cyber security approved and expert at delivering cloud storage to surpass expectations. We are trusted by hospitals, schools and quality manufacturing companies across the UK because we ensure that they can function safely 24 hours a day, on or off-site. Proud to be approved and partnering with credible, large organisations, we deliver the most effective, up-to-date IT solutions in the world, keeping our customers safe, operating, and cared for. Our ongoing review of all companies 'IT processes, from a disc drive to a cloud, delights directors who work with us and they continue to refer us.

Whilst I'm unsure if A Technology Company is exactly your cup of tea, would it be ok to book a Zoom call with you? From there, we can talk about care and cyber security then decide whether to schedule a deeper conversation and start planning. How about next Thursday at 3 pm?

Best wishes
Olly, A Tech Expert

Creating a library of strong email templates to send when you meet an ideal prospect is a good idea. Remember to personalise and avoid spraying emails to all and praying that some bite. Emails do have a place in the prospecting toolbox. Making the first email count matters as, unlike real life, you can be discarded into junk. Please remember to mix up the tools for the best effect.

19 Exhibitions

Sit down?

- Toby, what is wrong with this picture?

I show the room a picture taken at a huge exhibition in Manchester a few years ago. It is a stand showcasing high-end, big-name photocopiers. There are three people on the stand all behind the photocopiers, two are sitting down and one is leaning on the copier. They are all reading, scrolling on their phones, and eating lunch somewhat hidden behind the chap standing up leaning on the new state-of-the-art copier. The stand is ok, pretty standard, with pop-up banners, branded cups, pens and two copiers. This chapter in relation to prospecting has little to do with the stand design and layout. This chapter is about people and at this event a massive lack of prospecting activity, in fact, none. I took the picture, in full view and they were unaware, and still are. I use it regularly to show how not to prospect at an exhibition.

Many organisations waste money and miss prospecting opportunities at an exhibition. Why would you invest £5000 plus to be on a stand at a business exhibition and then sit down?

This is what happened at the major exhibition in Manchester.

I was excited to be going and had even used the online planner to work out who to look for, talk to and which workshops to attend, keen to learn more and meet new inspiring people. On arrival, the numbers seemed few, the atmosphere calm, surprisingly. Armed with the compulsory bag of brochure materials and a room plan, I entered the enormous venue.

Oh, dear! So many stands with people sitting down, reading, on phones and laptops or hidden behind the screen. I walked towards the workshop and passed many super displays and nobody spoke, smiled, or even acknowledged my curious glance. It would be great to be exaggerating but really this is exactly how it happened. Two guys I spoke with had hangovers, so were happy hiding! Two chaps without names badges or branding seemed happy to chat, but only when asked about their display. Talk about a missed opportunity! One lady smiled and approached me. One lady stood out in a hall full of business professionals.

Every stand displayed exciting content. Technology that can change how we all work. New apps, new systems, CRMs, time-saving, innovative things we should know about. The sad truth is that the opportunity to engage with a new prospect was missed by most as they sat down to read the paper and check their phones.

If you're attending or showcasing at an exhibition it is worthwhile knowing 81% of visitors are decision-makers. When this book is audible, please add the screeching noise and stop. That is a number worth repeating. 81% are decision-makers. Where else in a prospecting situation can you be so close to decision-makers? Ethel kept you talking eight times, hooks were left on voicemails, emails maybe read and networking, well you have been going for years. In this exhibition hall are your ideal prospects, the people you need to be in front of. Visitors at trade shows are often influential people within their companies, making these shows an ideal shop window. There are lots of opportunities for fresh prospects at trade shows, it is reported that over 64% will not currently be your customers. With 3% looking to buy today and 67% of the big fish in the next twelve months, this exhibition is an ideal place to be for a hungry, skilled, focused salesperson.

Not all trade shows are equal, but don't attend thinking you can just rock up, put a catalogue on your table with plain tablecloth and then sit down and wait for the magic to happen, it won't. To really maximise the incredible opportunity at an exhibition you need a plan, in fact, you need three plans, pre, during and post. Otherwise, you might become one of those companies claiming the exhibition did not work and omit to take any responsibility for why there were no results.

Before you exhibit, what is the plan? Many years ago, meeting a lady tasked with exhibiting at a local stadium, I asked her about the plan. She looked, smiled, and replied. "What plan Sally? Getting there will be an achievement!" Working with this company we sat down and began to create a plan that culminated in a checklist that still gets used today. The plan is to create a brand experience that is engaging, interesting, entertaining, relevant, personalised and **memorable**!

Memorable must be top of the list, remember if only 3% of people are ready to buy at the show and 67% are planning to buy in the next twelve months, what are you doing to ensure you are remembered, stand out, front of mind when they need what you do. Making memorable your objective is a good idea, for the right reasons of course.

Back to pre-planning, first, who else is going? An exhibitor list.

Toby looks up and asks, "I thought it was all about the visitors?"

Toby is right, the visitors are important, but so are the other exhibitors. Do any look like your ideal prospect, could they be referring you and you them, who will your neighbours be on the day? When you know who else is going, you can follow them and engage with their posts on social media. The interaction begins before the doors are officially open. Building familiarity and awareness ahead of the exhibition is a good idea. Will your company be remembered by as many businesses and decision-makers as possible? You can choose to plan to be memorable.

Using your company and personal social media, promote your attendance. Invite people to your stand, and share what you will be bringing, new products always go down well. When posting, tag the event organisers, having them in your corner can only help.

Know where your stand is located and how to get there. How will it look, be set up and packed away? What is the layout of the exhibition, who are you close to, where can you put your bags? All the details, if thought about now, will positively impact your return on time invested at the event. What will you be wearing, is there a dress code? Suit and tie, branded clothing, does everyone know? Have you got big, clear name badges so that people know your name without having to squint, save the job title for now, it is about you? Will you be taking business cards, using your phones or tech to save data? Are you staying over, is the hotel, transport and food booked? Are you staying where most other exhibitors are staying? Have you planned your journey, have others? Is there a plan B if anyone is unable to attend? Who is on the stand, is there a rota or agenda - a team brief planned, who is driving the day? Are your team familiar with the building, fire escapes, lift and car park?

What is on your stand to attract people? Planning this now is a brilliant idea. Toby shares how his company just have a table with a cloth and people sit or stand to talk about what they do. Toby's company are unsure about booking future exhibitions as they don't see the value! Many companies do just this and are missing a trick, forgetting the basics of sales that being liked and trusted comes first. Talking at a decision maker before beginning to build rapport, engagement or just a smattering of conversation will see them walk on by.

So, what is your hook on a stand? One company spent about £35 on a Tiddlywinks game, it was great fun and delivered engagement, with ROI huge. Passersby were invited to put the tiddlywinks in at the top and if it popped into the correct space, excellent, you would be entered into the draw to win. For even less money a medical supplies company filled a large glass bowl with blue sterile gloves. Passers-by had to guess how many gloves were in the bowl to be entered into a prize draw. The closest guess won. Guessing sounds, having a go at golf, and playing the game are all excellent ways to engage with your audience and are not SELLING! No one likes to be sold to, really, they don't. Most people do like to win, have fun or have a chat. Ensuring you have an attraction or hook be it simple or out their matters. It provides your team with something exciting to talk about with a stranger, a stranger who might just be a future client.

One of the most memorable stands, created by a company I worked with, involved Elvis - yes the king, the one and only. They put Elvis in a shower cubicle. An employee at the company happened to be a huge Elvis fan, knew the lyrics, and owned the outfits, he also looked spectacular. This was the year everyone would be talking about Elvis in the shower pod. The social media teased at his arrival and the pictures on the day were brilliant. Another client took tiny ponies to their stand, again, memorable. Be remembered for being a stand-out for all the right reasons. Will people be talking about your stand in a month's time? Probably not if it is a tablecloth on a standard table and most definitely if they got their photo taken with Elvis.

The most important part of pre-planning an exhibition, what is your goal is. Are you looking for brand awareness, familiarity, an increase in followers on social media? Is the measure footfall, the number of entries, face-to-face visits booked post-event, apps downloaded or sales? Being clear from the outset as to what your goal is will allow a clear measure of return on invested time and money. Before committing to future exhibitions, you will have a measure of which ones deliver results. Goals as a company and for individuals salespeople keep the focus on achievement. Be sure to have a category within your CRM noting where you first met your new prospect.

Each company's pre-event checklist will differ, creating this as a living document to be updated post-event works. All exhibitions are not equal and cutting your teeth at a local event is a great way to formulate plans for the future. When you're investing big money at a big exhibition with a slick, proven plan the results will be big.

During The Exhibition, don't be hungover. Arguably this should be common sense.

Back to the Manchester event. Towards the bottom of the huge exhibition hall was an energy stand, it was slick. Moving pictures of high-speed images, fuel, oil, and gas, grabbed your attention and was compelling. I went to have a look, smiled and oh dear, the young chap barely standing looked green. "Are you ok?" "Too many Jaeger bombs, knew it was a bad idea but we just kept drinking, only left the bar a couple of hours ago and now it's really kicking in, in fact, I'd better….." He dashed away hand over mouth in the direction of the toilets. His mate in branded clothing was left to hold the fort, oh dear. You could smell the alcohol from a distance, he looked half asleep and muttered something about a good night. He then suggested taking a leaflet before sitting back down behind the screens.

It is business, a venue packed with your ideal prospects is not the place to be hungover. It should be common sense, really it should. An exhibition can often be viewed as a jolly - show up, wing it and enjoy a hotel breakfast? More interested in the free bar than the return on investment. The young chaps I met had absolutely no chance of winning new opportunities and to be fair I doubt they cared. Maybe if their boss had been visiting or if it was their business, they might have viewed it differently.

If you like a drink, save it for post-event, many a relationship can begin in a bar. Save being drunk for another time, it is not cool.

At the event be proactive in your approach, stand up, reach out, and engage in conversation as people walk by. Compliment their shoes, suit, and coat - make it authentic and it will hook. Ask if they have entered the competition of the day. Invite them to have a go. Smile, smile and smile some more, remember the chapter on creating a fabulous lasting impression. Now is the time to bring all of that to the event. A smile is your power tool! Look the part, smart, fresh, and reflecting your company the right way. Be attentive, and focused on the task to hook people to your stand and begin conversation. Be memorable.

Being hungover is not a good idea on a stand, nor is eating. Have you tried to engage your ideal prospect whilst stuffing an egg sandwich in your mouth? It is not a good look. Go elsewhere to eat and check your phone, away from the stand. The notification about Beyonce's new hairstyle can wait, really it can. Stand up straight, and display polite, confident (not arrogant) body language. Be the one people want to speak to. Make your stand the stand everyone veers towards. If you are enthused, excited to be there, your passion for exhibiting will radiate and attract.

Bring out your true open questions, "Tell me about your day so far?" Use the compliment, get them talking and importantly when they ask what you never reply with … We do, our company does… make it about them.

Time to make it about your visitor. Imagine if the photocopier guys were approached and asked what they do. The standard reply is "We do photocopiers." Ok yawn, move on, next stand. "What do you do?" We do CRM." Yawn, next stand. "What do you do, actually never mind you look like you're about to throw up," and next stand?

The picture could look so different. Just imagine if selling copiers, when asked what you do your reply is, "Office managers call me to help keep printing and copy costs down." Or "Managing Directors have me on speed dial when looking for a reliable copier." Or "Forward-thinking procurement teams look to us for quality copiers in all their branches." Make what you do about them. Sadly, this is often replaced with a launch into a pitch, oh dear. Make it about them and remember rapport, be liked, and remembered. Time on banter, chit chat is well spent and if asked what you do make it relevant to and about, the person who is asking. Being remembered is easier if you talk about how you help companies and people who look just like your prospect. Recapping this in the planning stage is an excellent use of time.

Spark conversation with people who are walking towards you, be curious, dig deeper into their reply. Engage and then maybe they will be happy to have a picture taken on the stand or in the selfie frame. Take your photo frame or gimmick and share on LinkedIn if business, tag them, maybe connect there and then. All these tiny action points, these extra layers added together are fab and move you closer towards a visit, meeting or sale. Big fish remember?

In the early days of Fun Training for Results, while showing at an exhibition, I took a pink, branded photo frame. Everyone who passed and chatted was invited to have their picture taken. The uptake was vast and posted on LinkedIn soon after. The event was a success. A few weeks afterwards chatting with Martin from a communications company he made a comment, "Sally on the day of the event LinkedIn was packed with you, and for several days after." The irony being there were few pictures of me, they were all visitors to the stand. How powerful in business that well planned, you could dominate a social media channel positively for little money. ROI is huge, familiarity and awareness built, most definitely.

You will be meeting new people, maybe connecting, sharing a game, quiz, or a chat. Be sure to take notes. Noting down key points of information matters. If the day is packed, your feet won't hit the ground and remembering the name, likes and interests of the company director you met at 9 am will be a struggle by 5 pm, so write it down, this information is future gold.

The basics worth mentioning have a plan B. If someone does not arrive, who can step in and are they briefed? Is the tech working, checked, double-checked and where is the spare battery? Take an extension lead.

Your high heels might look great but worn for hours and hours will hurt! Think comfort. The world's finest airlines save the heels for arrival and departure only, the rest of the time they bring out the flats for good reason.

In your upbeat team brief before the day begins, run through health and safety, the rota for breaks and remember that when on their break the people in that event space are potential customers.

The checklist for when you are there should be a living document. As you attend various exhibitions your knowledge of what works well and less so increases, make a note, and learn for next time.

You have planned before the event and been brilliant at the event. You and the team are buzzing, met so many brilliant people and they all look like prospects. Sadly, this is where it ends for many. Head back to the office, unload the van and note you have 200 emails to answer, must go and see that client, the site visit is booked for tomorrow - normal begins again because you let it.

Post-event, the follow-up is the most important thing to do if you want a clear return. You have just 48 hours to make it count. Be extraordinary like On It Olly, clear your diary for two days post-event to follow-up, follow-up and follow-up.

First, the data, if you did not connect at the event on social media do so now. If the data is not in the CRM yet, put it in. Next a call, yes, a call, not the automated email that goes to everyone but a call from you a human, picking up after the exhibition and arranging a coffee, visit, next step. If the call remains unanswered, be persistent, then the email, but a personalised email, suggesting a coffee or visit or next step.

If they look like an ideal prospect, stand out and post a thank you card, again written by you, make it local, relevant, and fun. Do it now in the moment.

Pull out your notebook and make sure the details are noted on the CRM. Note who you meet, what was said and where. Revisit social media and check you have engaged with all the posts, tagged all the right people, and set a doorbell on the future posts of ideal prospects.

Thank the organiser. A card, email or on social media, remembering to thank them is good manners and keeps you front of mind for next year.

Within 48 hours schedule a team debrief. What worked, what could be better, what outcomes have you had and are forecast? At this point, plan your next debrief for a week's time. Make the measures in line with your individual and personal goals. Celebrate the success and build on this event for the future.

In business it is the follow-up that seems to be put to one side, maybe later, it can wait. Now is the moment to make it count, you're front of mind, on social media, at the event and now is the time to make a phone call. Maximise the moment and deliver a clear return. Avoid follow-up in the moment and you are wasting valuable prospecting opportunity, time and money.

As with the other stages, your checklist post-event needs to be living and a shared point of reference. What can be added to next time to make your return even better?

Become brilliant at prospecting at an exhibition! With a clear plan, exhibitions can deliver a phenomenal return when you do it right. They are an excellent tool to have in your prospecting toolbox.

Win business at exhibitions, have three plans and when there, stand up, smile, and begin a conversation!

20: Social Media

A fast-track way to build familiarity and awareness

Luddite **Larry** had been in Proactive Piers's sales team for over 17 years, he knew it all, had seen it all and felt that there was absolutely no need to change anything. All this social media stuff was killing time, showcasing your identity, opening you to potential fraud and ultimately for teenagers!

Piers and others in the team were curious about LinkedIn, so much so that with the help of several YouTube tutorials they set up profile pages, and a company page and began interacting. Piers swapped the drunk picture of himself at a wedding and replaced it with a professional shot, changing titles, making his contact details correct and reflective of his position in media. Using a background picture that reinforced what he sold and how he helped people. Rewriting his summary to include emojis and importantly help people understand how he could help them, following the process. Accumulating recommendations from happy customers, ensuring that the results of the media he sold were there as testimonials for all to see - particularly prospects. Piers began to post pictures, quotes, observations, clients, paying forward, and being consistent. It took time, as other LinkedIn users learned about Piers, they began to build a relationship with him and in time LinkedIn brought Pier's referrals. Being connected to the people he wanted to source, these referrals were high quality and they converted to big sales!

Piers now loves LinkedIn and uses it daily - ten minutes morning, at lunchtime, and afternoon. Growing his targeted network, being known, creating his own recognised profile, and awareness has created referrals for Piers. Larry, who for the past few years has kept his head firmly in the sand began to get twitchy. The MD at a sought-after company had called

Piers requesting a visit. Opportunities Larry believed to be a nonstarter were going to newer members of the team, helped by LinkedIn. Larry was losing his grip on being number one, he was uncomfortable, missing new opportunities, missing commission. Boozy lunches and back-slapping seemed to be delivering a poorer return. "Maybe," Larry thought to himself, "I should look at LinkedIn, maybe, but over a quick lunch with a bottle of Soave on expenses of course…."

I have met several Luddite Larrys over the years, resistant to change and with little recognition of how, if used correctly, it can be an incredible tool in a prospecting toolbox. The focus of this chapter is LinkedIn. In simple terms use the social media platform where your customers are., Be seen and found for what you do by the people with whom you would like to work.

If in business and looking for growth, to be like Larry and ignore LinkedIn is missing out on an opportunity. With over 34 million users in the UK and over 80% of business-to-business leads coming from LinkedIn, it is a powerful tool. When your prospects meet you or hear about you 76% will check you out on LinkedIn. The stats show that 57% will have decided if they make contact and do business with you based on your profile! With such incredible statistics demonstrating our reliance on LinkedIn as a research tool, not being there is missing out.

A quick trip back in time, about forty years to 1983. Remember the Yellow Pages advert for J R Hartley? A smart elderly gentleman is on foot trawling book shops in his area looking for a copy of "Fly Fishing" by JR Hartley. After visiting plenty he returns home without the book. His daughter encourages him to keep trying and to phone the bookshops listed in the Yellow Pages. Thanks to The Yellow Pages he calls a bookshop with a copy. The gentleman who happens to be JR Hartley is happy.

When working with organisations that have a Larry, this is a good analogy. Nowadays if we want to find anything we jump on to Google. In business, searching Google for an accountant in your area will bring results from LinkedIn. With limited knowledge of how Google works, SEO or any of the other mysteries around making you or your business found, in really simple terms, if you are on LinkedIn for what you sell or provide then you are more likely to be found. If not, chances are your competition will be.

Viewing LinkedIn as a directory is a good starting point. Is your listing reflecting who you are, where you work and how to contact you? It is that simple and no different to Meet The Team pages on many organisations 'websites. The beautiful thing I value about LinkedIn is that it is not a - 'look at me see how fab my life is, what I had for tea and my new shiny shoes 'social media platform. It is business and if you take time to look there is sensational shared content.

Before beginning to use LinkedIn as a prospecting tool, make sure your profile is set up correctly. Tips are below or there are some excellent trainers specific to this subject, Nigel Cliffe is easy to refer. LinkedIn has learning options and YouTube is full of people sharing how to set up a profile. Importantly if you believe you and your company's offering is top drawer, be sure to reflect this on LinkedIn.

Let's begin with your name. Make sure your name is the same name you use when meeting people. An example - if you're known as Vicky but your LinkedIn is Victoria - it can be tricky for people to find you. Your face needs to be about 80% of the picture and reflect the image you want to portray. Maybe move the bikini shot with a glass in hand back to Facebook unless you're a bikini model. Professional headshots really are worthwhile, with lighting, image, and a trusted expert to take the picture.

The banner behind your picture should be an image that showcases what you do and reflects the company. Your headline must share your key products so that if what you sell is searched for, you can be found. Importantly, and often forgotten, your contact details, work email, business phone number, landline and mobile numbers and business address. Showcase pride in your premises. Link to the company website, and social media feeds and importantly make it easy for clients and prospects to contact you. Link your skills to what you sell, note your certificates and accreditations, and build recommendations. Set your stall as number one and then when a prospect looks at you, they will be impressed and call. A final thought - if building a quality network on LinkedIn you might like to protect it. Making your connections only visible to you does exactly that and ensures that if a connection in your network becomes focused on new business development, they are unable to reach out to your network which has taken you years to build.

Social media is a powerful tool for gaining cold-calling inroads. With 82% of buyers believing a company or individual is more trustworthy if active on social media, using it is a good idea. Being active on social media in combination with meeting, calling, emailing, and attending exhibitions will in time see Ethel putting you straight through to your decision maker because they are familiar with you.

LinkedIn as a prospecting tool is a gift. In large organisations, sales navigator can deliver a clear return on investment. In smaller using the free offering is also good. Setting the doorbell on key prospects that you are targeting will notify you when they post. Advanced search enables you to search by job title, industry type, geographical region and even number of employees. It is a great tool that I would have relished back in the days of starting at A in the phone book!

Building recommendations is a good idea, calling ahead to request and signposting what you are looking for. Paying it forward and recommending is also a good idea. When you think a supplier or someone in your network deserves a recommendation, do it.

Toby has been quiet up until now, he then asks a common question that is frequent in training. "Sally, how do I know what to post?"

Posting on LinkedIn is a topic that can create debate, some do nothing, others post everything and some ad hoc. I suggest being in the habit of commenting on posts that you're interested in or value. Being authentic works in the long term. Share posts that have been created by experts with your network if you believe they will add value and not just because you feel you should or need to share. Become known for what you do and stay on topic. Highlight your keywords with a relevant hashtag #prospecting #salestraining #sales, three maximum and reinforce your area of expertise.

This is simply my opinion but sharing your deepest, darkest, inner secrets or what you had for lunch with a network who look to you for content about cyber security will confuse rather than look cool.

View LinkedIn as a prospecting tool, a superb way to build familiarity and awareness. Share content you believe could be valuable to others. If you're questioning why you are posting, maybe don't. I post #sallyfacts - tips to help people sell more and have happier customers. Pictures of teams in training having fun, learning lots, and smiling. The LinkedIn posts are frequent, consistent with the website and brand and importantly deliver value to others who choose to read, watch, or share. Toby could look at his company post and share his comment on industry news and create a post around the topic or share a podcast, Steven Bartlett has a thought-provoking variety within Diary of A CEO.

Simply, post and be seen, comment and share with your authentic comment and be consistent in your approach.

Out for a walk at lunchtime one day, I received a call from an incredible business leader. He said he had been watching and noting how I helped companies for about two years. He is a big fish; he did go slow. It was an absolute joy to work with him and his people. He called me because I use LinkedIn well and had built familiarity and awareness.

PART 3

THE SALES PROCESS

Part 3: The Sales Process

21 The Sales Process - Why?

This is it, the magic, the glue, the top sales tips, eagerly sought after. This is the bit where you learn to sell.

The irony is that whilst most people tend to want this part first, without understanding the importance of a sales mindset and knowing how to find people to sell to, a sales process is wasted, pointless in fact. Even worse, bringing new customers to a business that does not delight customers can leave a bad taste, see hard-won prospects walk and certainly no repeat business.

Walking with a friend I used the analogy of baking a cake. There's no point having the top-of-the-range mixer, pre-heated oven and a beautiful cake stand at the ready if you haven't bought the ingredients.

It is the same for selling. You need the ingredients first before opening the recipe book. You need to have your sales mindset, know your ideal prospect, and only when you find your ideal prospect, a sales process. A proven sales process that works.

So here we go, the sales process.

Using this process, following the steps in the correct order, will see you sell more. Follow the steps with an ideal-looking prospect and you are on to a winner, creating a future success story. Remember big fish go slow.

There are 11 steps to follow, and the next few chapters explore each one in detail. Learning them will require an investment of your time. Read and reread, complete the tasks at the end of each chapter and most importantly, practice.

It is worth remembering the stages of learning. Recall learning to drive? At this point in training, I invite people to step into their first car, buckle up and get ready to drive. The dramatics used is rather fabulous, mirror, and signal manoeuvre. Some people of a certain age must pull out the choke and have never had a sixth gear! Others turn on their Tesla by pressing a button on their phone. Relating the example to driving, and using the four stages of competence, I ask who recalls how they felt about driving a car before learning how to.

The first phase of learning to drive is when you look at others doing it, driving with ease and think this driving thing must be a doddle. At this moment you are **unconsciously incompetent**, you have no clue just how tricky this driving thing is.

Next, you book lessons, sit in the car and oh dear, so much to do, so many things to understand and all at the same time, panic! This is terrifying. You have moved with the help of a lightbulb moment into the next phase. Now you are **consciously incompetent**. You need to have this lightbulb moment before, with practice, moving to the third phase. With repetition, practice, and a commitment to learning slowly you begin to grasp the brakes, revs, gears, look back, signal, manoeuvre and eventually the parallel park. It is a considered approach; this phase is known as **consciously competent**. You must think about every moment in detail, it is a conscious behaviour. Fast forward thirty-plus years, well maybe not that long, and you drive home without a second thought, in fact, you vaguely remember the lights and are sure that you stopped and signalled. You are now officially **unconsciously competent**. Congratulations!

The thing worth noting is it takes time to go through the phases. It is exactly the same when learning to sell. Many think selling is a doddle, easy, a walk in the park. They apply for and land a sales role, coast for six months panic and then out. Poor employees operate the sink-or-swim approach, some swim and stay for a while most sink and add to a high churn rate for sales roles and

HR.

Really, selling is a discipline. Like dancing on Strictly Come Dancing, it looks graceful and maybe even easy but underneath is a huge skill set and a proven process that must be followed, otherwise you will stall, crash and burn (or should that be churn)?

Using a sales process, a set of repeatable steps will convert prospects into customers. A standardised sales process adds structure and accountability, leading to a higher success rate and shorter sales cycles. Knowing what needs to be done at each stage of the sale provides a huge advantage over salespeople like Wing It Wayne.

This process is for a sales call with a decision maker, it might happen over months or one meeting, and it might take moments or hours. This is business, not just a coffee or the easy chat with Ethel, now you are with the decision maker, or the team of decision makers and it matters. This is the opportunity you created from targeted prospecting, coffees, networking and sometimes years of nurturing. It matters, so let's get it right.

Back to Wayne, Wing It Wayne to his friends and colleagues. Throughout the sales process Wing It Wayne and his polar opposite On It Olly showcase how they approach the sales process across all eleven steps.

Wayne showcases horrendous and common habits used by really terrible salespeople. On It Olly, so cool that he can rock a lilac suit, used to be like Wayne but with 2008 and a hard recession he learned that to be number one in sales, a tenacious, hungry, and highly disciplined approach was needed. On It Olly is the company's top seller, he wins business and makes it look easy. Olly just follows a process and the sales follow.

As you listen to or read the chapter relating to the steps, begin to note what Wing It Wayne didn't do and what On It Olly did do that delivered completely different results.

22 Step 1, Plan and Prep

Plan More - Sell More!

You're ready! Your mindset is positive and your ideal prospect is identified. The prospecting strategy has paid off and you are booked to meet your future ideal customer.

At this point many sales reps chill, knowing the diary is full and their activity will be good, so something must land. It's just the numbers game approach. If, however, you are like On It Olly, this is just the beginning. Step 1.

Step 1 Plan and Preparation. Olly will clear maybe an hour in his diary and quietly focus on learning all about the prospect, shall we call him Bob? If Bob were to say yes, then the account could be worth thousands to his firm. Worth getting it right, and being prepared and ready.

Wing it Wayne will plan for a holiday usually a year in advance, he will plan for a lad's night out, a football game or a darts match. When it came to a stag do in Prague, Wayne's preparation was superb, yet when it is planning for a sales call, he did nothing, absolutely nothing and left it all to chance.

First things first, Olly worked out the numbers, approximate of course but understanding the return and value he could deliver to Bob, the potential solutions he could bring and the value they would deliver. Understanding the potential return meant that Olly could approach the meeting with absolute belief that his company, product and service could help Bob.

Next, the detail. Who else would be there? Had he looked on social media and the prospect's website? Was he familiar with their faces and would he be able to recognise and greet them if they walked through reception? Olly asked his network and colleagues if they knew of Bob and on occasion put in a call to a trusted, mutual connection. This info had proved invaluable over the years and led to Olly taking Jaffa cakes to one prospect. The first impression was positive and a nice touch that set up the meeting beautifully.

He spent time on Bob's website and socials, understanding the business, and its news and reading the Meet the Team pages. He checked for awards won and charity events they had signed up for. Companies House, DuDil and other financials were important as was looking at the company on his CRM, detailing any notes from previous meetings.

A tip Olly frequently used was pulling testimonials or recommendations from companies that looked like his prospect. Being able to share success from a similar-looking company was often a game changer and owning this was all part of great preparation.

Olly even planned the journey, noting the postcode, where to park as well, change for the machine (just in case) and journey time in rush hour traffic. Olly knew to factor in an extra half an hour just in case. He could always work in the car but being late was inexcusable. Olly would google image the premises and use street view, all to ensure he felt comfortable when going for the first time, the nerves removed as places looked familiar.

Olly had long ago created a plan and prep checklist and working through it ensured he was ready for his first call. Always ready and prepared, Olly knew life was sometimes unfair, a last-minute cancellation or change might happen. This led to him always having a plan B. If his visit were to change, he knew who to drop a surprise gift with locally. He had identified a new office open working space where future prospects might be or maybe even like he did at the beginning of his sales career, some in-person prospecting on the nearby industrial estate.

The detailed planning ensured an unsurpassable success rate.

The best part of Olly's planning, now that was his 'cheese'.

Toby had been quiet until now. "Cheese Sally, really, cheese?"
- Yes Toby, the cheesier the better and better still delivered with a twinkle in the eye and most importantly confidence. Cheese is so important - we plan it in Step 1, ready to deliver in Step 2

"So, what is cheese and how is it related to selling?" asks Toby.
- Cheese is when you pay the business that you are visiting or speaking with a compliment then you bring it back to how much better life will be when you are looking after them. An example - "Bob, your building business is incredible and your design innovation is impressive. With our tech support protecting your IT infrastructure you can rest easy knowing all your designs will be safe from attack."

It is cheesy, a compliment and a link to how your company can benefit, in this instance, Bob. Toby squirms.
"That is cheesy, Sally."
- Yes, it is and a note of caution, this cheese can only be delivered once. When meeting big fish, the same cheese on repeat will frustrate and annoy as opposed to impress and flatter.

Practice creating cheese, that is why it is in Step 1. It works.
"Why does it work?" asks Toby. For those who have completed sales training before I put the question back to them.
- What is happening when you deliver your cheese?

It takes a moment and then the penny drops. As well as paying a compliment you are assuming the deal. In the very first step, you are preparing to deliver an assumptive close. It is clever and effective but most importantly, requires you to have completed your math, the measure of return, and be confident about the solution you can bring and the value you can deliver. Cheese works if delivered with confidence and that comes from utter belief that you can help this prospect. In training, many cheese lines are created and shared for the cheeseometer rating! Companies create several and reinforce them in sales meetings, weekly training and 121s. Practice cheese with each other and see it land beautifully on a call.

Ahead of tasks, you might like to complete, enjoy the story about Wing it Wayne and On It Olly.

Wing it Wayne was a lad, a geezer, a fella who liked the banter, the laughter, and the ladies!

On a standard workday morning, Wing it Wayne flew by the seat of his pants smashing the alarm to snooze for the tenth time, taking a speedy shower, pulling on an un-ironed shirt and then a run for the bus. Usually, the later bus, squeezing in a hastily purchased coffee, Red Bull, and a boost bar. He would arrive at work on the dot, clock in, land on his seat and then breathe. He'd just made it!

Today Wayne was running late, standard some would say - well, his boss had said in his last appraisal. Wayne had been handed the lead of a lifetime. The Major Manufacturing Corporation is based in Leeds. This was better than his ideal client, their IT requirement could be huge, the opportunity massive. The pressure was on.

Wayne received the lead before Christmas and was due to meet live, face-to-face at their HQ in five minutes. Wayne was in a pool company car, stuck on the M1 with his sat nav showing 15 minutes at least until he reached Major Manufacturing. He began to sweat and hoot at the cars in front.

His phone was dead so he could not even put in a call. Twenty-five minutes later, Wayne arrived at the car park, found the only vacant, muddy parking space and ran across to Reception. Thirty minutes later a notably disappointed receptionist allocated him a badge and ushered him to the board room. Wayne was sweaty, shirt hanging out and trainers muddy.

The board room was immaculate. The leadership team including Bill Fates the IT director sat there looking equally immaculate. Wayne noticed their shoes gleaming. He had no idea who they all were or what job roles they held. In fact, he knew little about Major Manufacturing other than the address. He used the operation "Wing It" for most calls and it saved him so much time. Planning and preparation were so "last year".

He walked in boldly, hand on each hip, smiled and said, "Ey Up Lads, how are you?" Then he sat down without invitation and began to talk about his IT Technology support offering. He talked and talked, surprised that the board, especially Bill Fates, said nothing, so he kept talking.

Ten minutes in, they stood up, all at the same time and with a smile and a hint of disdain they walked out. Bill Fates walked out last. Wayne was sure he was tutting and then he said, "Make your way out." That was it, all done in under ten minutes.

Seriously, like this was all you got after sitting on the M1 for over half an hour and muddying up your new trainers? He was gutted - and asked to leave! Wayne sat in his car, perplexed by what had just happened. The lead was a dead cert. Really, to come away with nothing, no business card and no order - just a big, massive nothing!

Baffled, Wayne headed back to the office, the petrol gauge showed nearly empty. Never mind, that could be sorted out another time.

Olly glanced over at Wayne who had arrived back at the office before 11 am. Most odd as his call with Major Manufacturing was due to end at half past. The Major Manufacturing lead was a gift.

Olly was cool about Wayne receiving Major as he'd been given an opportunity with Maxim Manufacturing, their competitor based in Sheffield. The company was cool, using green energy to create recyclable packaging.

Olly spent a good two hours researching the company before the first meeting. The website, of course, the roles, news, and each person on LinkedIn. He reviewed Companies House, checked the accounts as well as asked the team and his bosses what they knew about this reputable company. That info had been invaluable, turns out the engineers used to work there and knew the team especially Elliott the IT director. Elliott had a fondness for Jaffa cakes.

Olly tried to understand the problems they might have, the opportunities he could bring and weaved an opening line around them, it was cheesy but effective. Planning to compliment Maxim on their innovation and how working with his tech company they could ensure all future secrets were cyber-safe. Very cheesy!

When Olly arrived, with Jaffa cakes, ten minutes early he took his time, heading to reception with five minutes to go. Ready to meet the team, having seen their faces online it was easy to say hello as he spotted Elliott in the reception area.

Elliott showed him to the board room and accepted the Jaffa cakes with a smile. Conversation was easy, about the building, holidays, and family. Building common ground, mirroring body language and matching words. Rapport was being built. Olly checked everyone was present and that they had the authority to proceed if they liked what he could offer, they did and so he continued.

Before any questions Olly signposted, stating the meeting would take no more than an hour and, in that time, he wanted to really understand what Matrix Manufacturing was looking to achieve, any problems to solve or even establish opportunities for them. Olly, referring to his notebook, said he'd be writing down their replies and he would confirm a date to return and present if he believed his company could help. Checking they were all happy, the call continued.

Ninety minutes later Olly drove back to his HQ knowing his return to Matrix was next week. The team were keen and ready to buy, his next job was to send an email to say thank you then it was time to create a perfect IT solution for them.

Olly loved his job, within a minute of being back in the car he got a text from Elliott - good to meet today, look forward to seeing how you can help Matrix in the future.

Wayne and Olly continue to showcase how to and how not to apply steps of sales in future chapters. Now take time to help step 1 stick and complete the tasks below.

Tasks:
* Create your own plan and prep checklist
* Create at least three examples of cheese.
* Time block an hour to plan and prep for your next call. It might take less time but an hour or so is a good beginning.

23 Step 2, Intro & Empathy

People buy from people they like and trust.

Step two of the sales process sees you with your prospect, on-site, on a call or Zoom. Here is the moment you have been waiting for.

Regardless of the location, a smile first before a word slips out of your mouth. Smile and be liked. Not a fake smile, a Duchenne smile, where your whole face, especially the crow's feet, (we all have them), ignites. This first, genuine smile will set you up in seconds to be liked.

Introduce yourself using your name twice and the company. This might be your first meeting of the day and you of course are all prepared but for your client, they might be on back-to-back meetings, so be clear, setting context is a good idea.

Now to build rapport. So easy to say and often so tricky to do. Chit Chat and banter are all rapport, they are easy ways to build a feeling of commonality quickly.

A note of caution, remember big fish go slow and read the body language. Rapport with a big fish might be swift as they are less interested in banter and more interested in getting down to business, time is precious.

This is absolutely not an ok to bypass building rapport. A feeling of commonality, feeling you are alike, on the same page and wired the same way in the early moments can see engagement skyrocket. Did you read the Culture Code by Daniel Coyle, about the experiment at a rainy station? Simply by apologising for the weather when it was raining the number of phones lent increased by 422%! Rapport matters and despite the many LinkedIn profiles or CVs stating "I am a natural rapport builder" building rapport and learning how is a skill and takes practice.

Rapport takes time, a commitment to being interested in others and the ability to politely get over yourself. Being awkward in front of others is how life rolls, especially when we are younger. Is that person judging how I look, my shoes, presentation, conversation, where I am from and the list goes on? Walk into a call with hangs ups and packed with self-doubt and standby for a crash and burn.

You see the amazing thing about people is that they (including you and me) are mostly preoccupied by themselves. That's right themselves, their life, their business their own self-doubt. With absolutely no time to be interested in anything other than themselves, you are walking into a call thinking they are judging or assessing you is a massive waste of energy.

Toby is back and looks puzzled, "So we now know that the person we are seeing is only interested in themselves, but how does that help me build rapport?"

Toby's question is great and often overlooked in training and sales courses. Rapport is talked about but how do you do it?

First, you put yourself into situations where there will many people you do not know. Networking is a great place to start. With the choice of sitting in a room alone or making yourself say hello, knowing that your boss is looking for results and new contacts, you get up and say, "Hello".

This might make you squirm and feel uncomfortable, even the thought of walking into a room full of strangers makes you cringe. Rapport is a skill and to build a skill takes time. This skill also requires confidence and confidence comes when we push ourselves into new experiences. Oddly, the more we push ourselves the easier it becomes. You might never become the Tony Robbins of the world and walk into a room and captivate that audience, that is ok. Being able to have a conversation with a stranger requires confidence and a positive mindset and that comes with practice.

"Sally. How do you build the rapport though?" asked Toby, looking a tad exasperated.

- There are five tips Toby. Firstly, do as they do, mirror, and match the body language of the person you are with. If they stand you stand, if they sit, you sit, if they are speedy in conversation and passionate share the passion and speed. If they talk about awesome, innovative, and unique, use their language in your words. Mirror and match what they do and speak.

Toby is laughing and says, "That will look so odd Sally, really odd."

Toby is right. Trying too hard to mirror or follow what the other is doing can look super weird. This rapport thing is a skill and takes practice. The great news is that when we like, know and trust someone, we naturally without thinking mirror them. Brew in right hand, hand in pocket, we match how they speak, their language and how they stand. Trying, (not too hard) to emulate this when building rapport is a good idea and puts the other person at ease. After all, you look and sound just like them, and they are mostly all about themselves.

Next, when building rapport be sincerely interested in whom you are meeting, really, truly, sincerely interested. You have by now done thorough planning and preparation so make it count. Be ready to listen without "But", share their space, use eye contact, and avoid the disruptive ding. Every salesperson should know how to put their phone on silent, turn notifications off and better still leave the phone, mac or tablet away from this meeting. Two people talking to each other, beginning what could be a lifelong business relationship is way too precious to disrupt with a ding, phone going off and "Oh sorry" as you fumble in your bag to turn it off. Watches with messages that flash up fall into the same category, it is ill-mannered to be looking at a message on your watch. You might as well say to your prospect that you are interesting but not as interesting as the fascinating email that just popped up on my watch or the message from the car park attendant regarding a fee increase. Turn everything off, be sincerely interested, take an hour or maybe more and make it count. Take notes, accept a brew, and enjoy a tour around the factory. Give 100% of your focus and attention to your prospect. Your prospect who, remember, thinks that they are the most important person in their world, will relish the attention, that someone else recognises how important they are. You are two steps into building excellent rapport.

Next, pay a compliment, and make your prospect feel good. Warning, walking into a room, sidling up to the brand-new acquaintance, leaning in and enthusiastically sniffing their neck before looking them in the eye and saying, "Wow you smell amazing!" could most likely see them bring a meeting to an abrupt end. Pay authentic compliments and make them less awkward by backing up with a question. "You smell great, what fragrance are you wearing?" Is less likely to see you receive a complaint and a quick end to a call. Great reception area, lovely car, shoes, whatever it is, find something to compliment. Make people feel good and they will like you, which in case you have forgotten, will fire up that good old limbic brain, storing all the likes. Bringing you one step closer to a yes!

Rapport requires you to build common ground. It is after all a feeling of commonality. The phrase 'birds of a feather flock together' is a great reminder. We tend to stay around and do business with people we feel are like us. How to build common ground takes thought, especially if you are polar opposites, in age, lifestyle, culture etc. so it is your job to make it happen. Look at where they live, their location, age, are they likely to be watching Strictly or Love Island? They most likely eat so talk food, restaurants, health fads, whatever the common ground, find it and use it. When training young teams, the question is often, how do I build common ground with someone, a business leader who could be my grandad? Geography is an easy one, so use it. Being based in Oxford is a gift, a stunning part of the world, it is on my list of places to visit, and so is Nottingham, Derby, Glasgow, and the list goes on. As with all rapport, practice and more practice will see you improve and refine this skill.

Body language matters. Don't try to build rapport with a stranger if you're stood up and they are sitting down, you have your arms so tightly wrapped around you it resembles a straight jacket, your legs crossed, eyes down and, well, everything is down. This body language is a massive sign saying, "Closed!" Be open to chat, stand up, face forward, hands to the side, shoulders back and head up. If the thought of this makes your tummy turn maybe watch the incredible Ted talk by Amy Cuddy that talks about faking body language until you become it. It's very good.

Toby says, "It is often cold Sally, so I like to keep my hands in my pockets." It is a comment I hear frequently. Maybe Toby has particularly cold hands, but you should realise hiding your hands suggests you are hiding other stuff and keeping hands visible suggest transparency and being open and given this is about building rapport to be liked and trusted - then take the hands out of the pockets!

Rapport is one part of step 2. Next and most importantly, are you with the decision maker?

Your plan and preparation are about the decision maker and their business. Targeted prospecting of the business and the decision maker have led to this call happening. Now you are there, at the beginning of the meeting and it is prudent to double check you are with the decision maker and ask if anyone else needs to be invited to the meeting. You might have done this ahead of time and all the signals are good but still, you arrive to meet a couple of extra people joining in the meeting. No need to panic, breathe and say hello, note their names and roles. If your planning was thorough, you have most like seen them on LinkedIn or the company website. Most importantly, double-check, simply saying, "Before I start taking notes would it be ok to check that you make the decisions, or might it be prudent to invite others?"

Many years ago, as a media field sales rep, targeted prospecting and persistence earned me a call with the MD of a prestigious media agency in Ilkley. Diary invites were accepted, all the right signals were received, the plan and prep were done, and I was ready. Arrived in good time, parking close to Betty's tea rooms, in case plan B was needed, then walking to the appointment. On arrival, smiling at the receptionist building rapport and stated I was there for a meeting with the MD. She glanced down, then looked at me apologetically! That look said everything. "Oh, well the MD said he was too busy, **but** it is ok he has arranged for you to meet with Luke." Luke, I had no recollection of a Luke, so I enquired "And Luke's role is?" "Oh, he is the new apprentice, he joined just this week and is on induction."

Recall the phrase, everything before the "But" is bull shit? It certainly was here, in a moment I understood the MD had no intention of meeting, filling Luke's induction was on his agenda. This MD had no understanding of the value of the service I was selling, or how it could maybe help his business. If he did understand, he definitely had no intention of talking it through with me today although he was happy for me to contribute to Luke's induction with a business meeting!"

What to do? Stay and play ball, and carry out your next steps with the brand-new apprentice who has absolutely no buying authority, influence or, after just a couple of days, understanding of the company vision, opportunities or problems that could be remedied. That would be a waste of time and as with all sales reps, time is precious. Politely I turned to the pleasant receptionist, thanking her for the information and politely suggesting I reschedule with the MD rather than waste anyone's time. Part of plan and prep was a plan B, so I went to take Bettys Fat Rascals to an existing client, as a gift, just because. They were surprised, and happy and continue to refer.

The receptionist was a little shocked and remained apologetic, maybe even embarrassed. As I walked out another rep walked in, I heard him apologising for being early and that he had an appointment with the MD. I wonder if he stayed. The meeting never happened; I never met the apprentice. Years later I meet the MD at a networking event. With no memory of the failed meeting he shared how business was tricky, finding staff hard work and apprentices, well, they seemed to stay a minute or two and go. I smiled and moved on.

Just the cheese left to deliver. Ok, so the flow of step 2 will most likely be different, after all, you are looking to have a conversation, not work through a checklist. When walking around include the cheese, "Your offices look stunning, the revamp sets the tone of high quality and forward-thinking, when working with Toby's Print your literature will reflect your business beautifully, and everyone will be talking about you!" Toby liked this cheese!

Cheesy but if delivered with a smile, a twinkle in the eye and the utmost belief that when they use what you have to offer then the magic will happen.

You have probably only arrived at cheese if your first impression was a good one. Maybe refer to a Fabulous First Impression in Ch 7.

Step 2 is complete, can you see how Wayne got it so wrong in the story in chapter 23? In Step 2 take time to build rapport, deliver your cheese and check you are with the decision maker. Then you're ready for Step 3.

24 Step 3, Signpost

If a situation is unclear, it's uncomfortable.

This morning it's foggy, dense fog. Throw in the early morning darkness and visibility is low. You can see a little way in front of you, but the whole distance, no chance. There is a low light, a fuzzy glimmer from a streetlamp but that is it. Having repeated this walk many times makes it a little easier but if this was a first, you'd be lost, most likely uncomfortable, a bit worried and maybe even scared. How will you get there? Where is there? Does it have an end, how far is it, and will there be obstacles? So many questions that if answered would contribute to dispelling the uncomfortable feeling.

When you can see the destination clearly, and know where you're going and what the outcome will be, then life is sweet and your mind is open to new ideas.

This analogy is perfect for Step 3 in the selling process, "Signposting". Often forgotten, bypassed for a launch into endless rapport or an uninvited demo. Signposting is a tiny step in the process, a magic bullet. Miss it and the whole sales call can be ruined.

A few years ago, I was lucky to be shadowing an experienced rep called Tim, Talkative Tim. He had a qualified appointment with the decision-maker at a reputable car dealership. Arriving in good time, plan and prep done, the rep greeted the car dealer, Lawrence with warmth, maybe too much warmth if that's possible. I sat there listening on the pretense of learning the ropes. They talked football, cars of course and Hearsay, (it was a band at the time). From the sidelines I could sense Lawrence was getting fidgety, looking at his watch several times and ushering Tim towards his desk.

Lawrence sat behind his desk with Tim opposite; I watched. Lawrence said, "Well?" Tim replied, "Yes, thank you but a brew, strong white, three sugars would be nice." Lawrence stood up and went out. We were twenty minutes into an allocated one-hour meeting. Tim made himself comfortable and when Lawrence returned with his tea, he totally missed his frustrated expression. "What did you think of the match last night then, Lawrence?" Lawrence shuffled in his chair and replied, "Shall we talk business?" "Oh, of course" replied Tim who then sat up, opened his presentation, and began to share slides 1, 2 and 3 with Lawrence. With passion, Tim shared about his company values, the car park, the history of the CEO and the number of awards they had won in the last twelve months making a point of sharing the photos of himself holding the award.

Lawrence had dragged his chair out and back, hanging onto the arms of his seat as he looked ready to run. He was a big fish, this meeting, 50 minutes on, was at slide 3. All he wanted to know was whether their software could help him. Lawrence looked to Tim and asked about the software. Tim, mid-flow and annoyed at being interrupted showed Lawrence the hand and with vaguely disguised diplomacy said, that would follow, page 52 to be exact.

Lawrence moved the chair back even more, stood up turned to Tim, apologised then explained about his next meeting - and he was gone, out of there! Lawrence never spent money with Tim or his company. Never again did Tim or anyone from his company get invited back. The call was a disaster, Tim had completely missed step 3, Signposting.

Instead, if Tim had speedily mentioned how he would take no more than an hour, ask questions about Lawrence's business today and in the future with a view to confirming a return date to present possible solutions; that he would be taking notes and checking if the time frame suited, then that could have been a fruitful call. Tim didn't do that, and he missed a trick and any future sales opportunity.

Clear signposting, putting people at ease, is key to making people feel (limbic brain relaxed) happy. As human beings we like and value being able to see and know what is happening next, to see how it looks, where the destination is. We like to know how to get from the airport to the hotel, from the lobby to the gym equipment, and where to store our phone and kit. When starting a new job we want to know how long induction will be, where the loos and fire escape are. It is knowing all the small details that can put us at ease and it is not knowing that makes us feel uncomfortable.

In training I share a story about opening a first-ever business bank account. It was a big deal, a first ingredient in beginning a new adventure, being in business. The appointment to visit the notable High Street bank was for Saturday 9.30 am.

Fortunately, the Friday before, I was with a group of successful businesspeople on a coach to York Races. York Races with hospitality does not necessarily require you to drink Prosecco on the coach before 10 am but, well, it had been a great year. At the races we were offered champagne, Prosecco, lobster, crab, prawns, everything available for the taking when it came to drinking and eating. It was the races but trying to walk to the course in heels? A silly idea so you stay put, take another sip, and give your bet to the kind man walking around and hope that choosing a horse name that reminded you of a song back in the day would secure a win. To be honest it was a pointless task, by the end of the racing most of us were in no state to note who had won and not a hope of collecting any wins. Instead, we staggered back to the coach looking rather less glamorous than we did on arrival. Singing, backsides out of windows (it was a thing on old coaches with windows that opened) and very funny stories that seemed even funnier when well-oiled. On our way home the suggestion of more drinks met with a huge cheer and applause.

A tiny part of my brain suggested this was a very bad idea, I had to be at the bank in the morning. Tea, toast, and Emmerdale would be a much better plan. Ignoring that part of the brain, I headed into town with this brilliant team to party.

The next morning! You can only imagine, somehow my husband and I arrived at the bank. I wanted coffee, cake and to be asleep. Instead, we made our way to the very trendy-looking bank. Modern counters, glass panels and pictures of fields on the walls to suggest the countryside and fresh air. I wanted coffee! The lady ushered us into an office with more pictures of cows and fields. She said nothing. Really, she said nothing. She sat down and started typing, her screen bleeped and more typing. She typed and said nothing. We sat, watching. My husband, a very nice man, noted at the 18-minute point my disgruntled expression. He gave me that kick, not a real kick but a kick that said take that look off your face and smile. I wanted coffee and cake. The bank lady said nothing. By 40 minutes even my very patient husband was beginning to look fed up. Then the printer kicked into action and spat out two pieces of paper. The bank lady stood up and wait for it, she spoke. "Can you sign here!" We did and then were gone. It was over.

Coffee and cake followed, just not at the bank.

How different the whole experience could have been if the welcome had been warm, and the rapport built followed by guidance such as that today's meeting will take no more than an hour during which I will be busy typing and saying little; towards the end I will ask you to sign some papers and then we will be done for today. Bank books will follow in the post. If she had calmly signposted and maybe added in "Grab a coffee or cake and maybe a sleep, Mrs. Roberts, you look like you need it!" that would have been helpful. At least we would have known what was happening.

As a salesperson, when you signpost the call, coffee, or meeting then you are in control of the direction it goes in. You put your prospect, colleague or other person at ease and make them feel (limbic brain) comfortable. Clear signposting ensures the person you're meeting with does not build cortisol waiting and wondering what will happen next. Noting time frames of no more than hour is a good idea. Too fast, just a few minutes and you can devalue the call, too many and you can see yourself without a meeting.

Importantly, when signposting it is critical to share what you're looking for at the end of the call, to diaries a meeting with a proposal, to ask for a decision to confirm the follow-up conversation. Toby has been quiet until now.
"Why is this so important, Sally?"
- Well, Toby, if you spend quality time learning about your client or prospect and want to go back to present, without a date in the diary you are allowing the competition to sweep in before you. If working with a top client, having frequent review meetings all about them, not you, in the dairy helps to lock them in and prevent your competition from opening a door. Dates in diaries cement relationships and leave your competition outside.

Signposting makes meetings for both parties clear and comfortable, a great lead into step 4 of the selling process,

Did you note how On It Olly clearly signposted the call, far slicker and more professional than Wayne?

25 Step 4, WHATSAS

Knowing it "all" creates opportunity.

Step 4 of the sales process is sometimes known as a fact find, need find or uncovering the gap is WHATSAS. It is a list of letters to prompt you to remember the questions in order. What, How, Area, To Whom, Special, Anything Missed and Summary!

Remember Tim, the salesperson who bypassed signposting and launched into a pitch? Tim is textbook. He does what many new salespeople do. Often it stems from his induction at a new company when, even before arriving, he has genned up on the new company he is about to join. Then on Day One he meets others who share about the company. His induction, lasting two weeks, sees him spend a day in all departments of said new company to learn about what they all do and how. Two weeks in and Tim is now super knowledgeable about the company to the finest detail, even knowing how to mix printer inks that he is never likely to mix. HR think a fab induction has been completed. The sales manager thinks an excellent induction has been done so now Tim, the new guy, will be ready to sell.

AAAAHHHH! Seriously what happened? You joined to sell the product or service this company has and in a whole two-week induction not once did you meet a customer to find out what they buy or most importantly why they buy.

Momentarily let's flip the induction for beginning a new role in sales. On day one complete the HR and payroll bits and then from day two you are off meeting at least two of the company's customers a day, going out with the existing, successful sales team. This completes after two weeks and your knowledge of why people buy and what they buy is top-notch. You now know from the customers 'perspective why they love working with your company, and the many problems your company has solved and is looking to solve in the future. Better still the same customers have shared opportunities that your company's product and service have helped them create.

So, you might not know how to mix a printer ink colour or the exact detail of the software but, so what? You don't need to. Your company hires a talented team full of experts who can answer those questions. Your remit is to sell, delight customers and ensure they are happy with problems solved, opportunities created and most likely referring you.

Induction at a company can be an opportunity and often it is omitted, viewed as an inconvenience, and replaced with a tick box exercise.

Tim, unaware of a sales process and in particular Step 4 WHATSAS, launched straight into what is often known as the show-up and throw-up. He began talking at Lawrence, he began pitching without any knowledge of what problems his prospect might need solving or opportunities he might need creating. Tim, with passion and gusto, went full throttle into a tirade of detail, the car park, fish tank and even the spec of the new office layout. He talked from a first-person perspective about how he could bring new ink, exciting software, how the company had lots of ideas and their many awards. It was cringeworthy and just like Wing It Wayne, he was demonstrating how to be ineffective.

A favourite story of why creating a need, finding a gap, identifying problems, and noting where opportunities can be created is written in Steven Covey's famous book, 'Seven Habits', when he talks about the opticians. In training, I ask someone who wears glasses to step up and pretend to visit Sally's Opticians. It is role play, fun and usually acted out on some odd-looking hotel carpet and it goes like this.

"Hello, welcome to Sally's Opticians! How may I help you today?"

They say, "I'd like some new glasses, please."

Excellent idea! Then I take my glasses from the top of my head and hand them to the person pretending to look for new glasses.

They pull a face.

"What's wrong?" I inquire.

"Well, umm, they won't be right, will they? I mean they are your glasses, for you."

"How rude!" I reply, "They are excellent glasses, fashionable rim and top-grade lenses, most people would be over the moon to have these glasses."

It's feeling uncomfortable as they squirm and say they will leave it for now and walk quickly out of Sally's Opticians.

Of course, it's fun and receives lots of laughs. It is also massively effective when landing the message that you need to know what your specific client's or prospect's problems are and how you can help them create opportunities.

In the 1980s the classic "ABC - always be closing" was bandied around as if it was a fabulous way to sell. Maybe it was if all you wanted was a sale there and then, a transaction. If, however, you're looking for a relationship, to work with a partner long term, then being in their corner means understanding the whole picture not just the first need and a quick close. Remember, big fish go slow and WHATSAS with some digging deep thrown in will uncover the whole picture. Only then are you able to pitch specifics that your prospect needs and wants?

Step 4 of the sales process is sometimes known as a fact find, need find or uncovering the gap. This is your opportunity to learn what problems the prospect might need solving and what opportunities you can create for them. This step is critical if you want to sell anything, you need to uncover problems you can solve or opportunities you could bring. WHATSAS is brilliant and with the correct questions will deliver you step 5, a gap to pitch to in step 6.

Before jumping into WHATSAS, understand that using the right question at the right time matters. **Questions** could be their very own chapter, but for now, the focus is three types. In networking, and building rapport with Ethel, one brilliant way to encourage conversation is by beginning with "Tell me…" or "Share with me…"

In training, the exercise takes a minute and can feel uncomfortable. Toby volunteers. The pretext being is that I have never met Toby, ever. He stands opposite me, and I begin. "What do you do?" Swiftly followed by, "Why do you do that?" Then quickly into "Where do you do that?"
Then, "How do you do that?" Next, "When did that begin?" and "Why that way?" "Who else do you work with?" Most likely the conversation stalls about here. Toby looks exasperated and says, "Wow, Sally, back off." Exactly the right response!

Toby happily shares how it felt awkward, uncomfortable, like a barrage of questions, an interrogation, and I don't know you.

Toby is exactly right; it would have felt that way because it was a barrage of questions. Often salespeople are taught to go and ask open questions, they might even take in a list, a crib sheet and off they go beginning at number one. Oh, dear!

Open questions are superb in a sales call. They get to the point, allow you to dig deeper and discover consequences if nothing or everything changes. Open questions are efficient.

True, open questions reserved for networking, strangers and a fast-track way to build rapport are beautiful, just not necessarily on a sales call. The exercise is replayed, still with Toby. "Tell me about yourself, share your plans with me." They are lovely, soft slippers of questions. These open questions also come with a warning. Used incorrectly they could see the person you address talking for hours about her cute cat, Billy the budgie and then onto her ailments before sharing her viewpoint on Saturday's Strictly and all because you asked her to share or tell. True, open questions have a place but if your sales call is booked for an hour, make it count and use open questions to get to the point.

Remember how Toby felt it was an interrogation and with good reason? It is important to use open questions conversationally. Weave them in as you tour around the showroom, add notes to your notebook, listen to the answers and be sure to listen without 'but', be curious, dig deep and avoid quick-fire, one after another after another. It takes practice, so practice, all those just coffees, 121's or follow-ups, practice using open questions relating to what you're looking to find out. Keep practising until they flow with ease.

This time two volunteers are needed, pre-warned they need to become a famous person, preferably somewhat obscure. Then they each need to become that person for a minute without sharing to the rest of the room. The others in the room are then divided into two teams. The instruction to team one is that in just sixty seconds they must guess who the first famous person is. To do this, they must ask only closed questions, a question that simply receives a yes or no answer.

Rarely do they find out who the famous person is although there is always plenty of laughter.

The second team then have sixty seconds to find out who the second famous person is. Their brief is to use only open questions, questions that receive a detailed reply, the opposite of yes or no. For example, what, where, how, who and maybe, why?

Team two usually find the answer in about, 54 seconds, often there is thunderous applause for their team's achievement. Oddly when team two begin to consciously think about the open question it feels robotic, odd that we tend to default to closed questions,

The "Uhm, really?" moment is when asking the teams how quick it could be to find out who each person was and suggesting just a second or maybe two. Met with puzzled looks, I turn back to person one and ask, "Who are you?"

This task showcases brilliantly the importance and efficiency of open questions. Use them wisely, follow WHATSAS, dig deep and you will establish Step 5 - your gap.

Before looking at WHATSAS here's a thought that I have found to be true. Rarely if ever do we like being told what to do. As children we take it, listen, and crack on because the teacher said so therefore, we must obey. In business and as we get older being told what to do immediately sets off the system one brain that wears trainers, gets our backs up.

Just imagine you are told what to have for tea, where or how to sit. Our default setting is, "No". Given that you are looking to ignite your prospects 'brains positively and have a delightful sales call, avoid at all costs telling them what to do.

Toby raises his hand, "Sally, I thought we were on the fact find, need finding part of the sale and I would not tell a prospect what to do". Toby makes a good point, we are in the fact find part and most salespeople have no intention of telling a prospect what to do, it just happens that the consequence of not asking enough questions is telling.

- Toby, imagine if we were to meet and before knowing anything about your business I begin to pitch, maybe out of courtesy ask a couple of questions and then because I have been selling to companies that look just like yours for many years, I assume I know what you want. Bypassing the questions in a manner that fails to establish the real need, problem or opportunity is no different to telling a prospect what to do.

Often salespeople that have been doing it for years will have extensive industry and product knowledge and they most likely do know what solution will fit the prospect, but to assume is a huge mistake. Every client or prospect thinks they are different, and many strive to be. Assuming you know what, they want before asking is a fast-track way to see them walk away. Who likes (limbic brain) someone that tells them what to do without asking? Remember it is the limbic brain that makes decisions based on like and trust. Ask more and sell more, providing you listen that is. Interestingly buyers when asked said they would be more likely to buy if they felt listened to. So, just a thought, ask questions, say less, and sell more.

"I love WHATSAS, Sally!" "When you understand the power behind it - boom wow, it is incredible, and it works." "Sally, this is the gold in your training."

WHATSAS is often met with mixed emotions. When introducing for the first time WHATSAS is met with nods of approval, of course, it makes sense, a great idea. Then, when we begin to use it, the reality of staying on track, jumping to the future, and avoiding pitching or worse trying to close rises to the surface, these are sales habits often created over years, so it makes sense.

WHATSAS is simply a pneumonic, a list of letters to prompt you to remember the questions in order. What, How, Area, To Whom, Special, Anything Missed and Summary!

Asking **What** questions, then **How**, then **Area**, next **To Whom** followed by **Special** and **Anything Missed**. to deliver your **Summary** or the gaps which is Step 5 of the selling process. For now, the focus remains on the questions.

- Toby, maybe when working through this exercise you might want to look at the document that lays out WHATSAS.

"What?" is a great beginning question albeit with caution. You have completed Step 1, your plan and prep, so going in and asking, "What do you do?" as if you haven't a clue is a bad idea. Ask, "What in their words do they do? What is the turnover, margin, range, average value order, most popular, and most troublesome? What provider do they use currently, and what do they like about them? What do they like less?"

If you are nervous about talking money, you might like to jump to the money talk chapter.

Before jumping to "How?" let's spend a moment on this question. Most likely, your prospect currently has a provider, a way of solving their problems or a trusted partner. Your persistent prospecting has created an opportunity to be in front of the decision-maker with your solutions. Asking what they use currently to solve their problems is a great idea. Next, the magic, ask what they like less about their current solution provider. Listen, take notes and smile.

For example, "What current tech solution do you use?"

The reply might be, "We use ABC1 tech software and have done it for years, an old IT director introduced it, but he is retired now."

"What do you like about ABC1 software?"

"It just works, it has been here for years, so the team know how to use it, it's easy."

"Software being easy to use is important. Out of interest what do you like less about the software?"

And off they go, sharing about the flaws, the reports it won't run, the data it won't store and the clunkiness of sharing images.

This is a real gem of a question if delivered with sincere curiosity and not an opportunity to slate the competition.

Toby looks up, "So you're suggesting we mention what or who they use currently in the fact find, that we mention the competition? Surely, we should avoid talking about the competition at all costs and stay believing in our product?"

Toby states what many salespeople think, that talking about the competition is a bad idea. Remember big fish go slow? A big fish will most likely have a tech provider, a supplier or software in place. By asking positively and keeping the language upbeat, 'like less 'as opposed to 'don't you like' or 'what doesn't it do' is keeping the prospect's system one brain chilled and happy to share.

The information shared prepares you for later in the sales call, Step 6 your pitch. The flaws mentioned now will be highlighted as wins with your solution. Or, of course, you could bypass this question and have less super-important info.

Now for the "How?" questions. How do you create results, manufacture, create opportunity, use the IT, software, grass seed or whatever it is you can ask around a "How" question? How do you source new suppliers, partnerships, and solutions? How are you marketing, promoting, and creating opportunities? The list could be endless and the exercise after this training module is to create a list of 64 questions minimum using WHATSAS.

Area questions follow. "What area of the UK do you trade in? What area of the market do you operate in? What is your area of speciality?" "What area of the building do you train, and keep your IT, cars, and software?"

"Who do you sell to, provide a service for, sell a product to? Who is your customer, internal and external? Who uses your software, tech training room? Who is your ideal client?" "Who?" is a hook to create specific questions that will keep you on track.

Now for "Special"! What makes your company so special? This question is gold and can see the prospect tell you plenty especially if their buying motive is pride. Sit still, listen and remember to mirror and match. Be excited about their replies, this is their moment. Frequent replies are the teams and the people, the product or service range and of course their company's dedication to customers. Take notes and smile.

The most important question about anything missed removes possible objections later on. As you are noting everything down you look up smile and say, "Thank you for such useful information. Is there anything else that maybe I have missed asking about?"

"Anything Missed?" is a beautiful question that suggests you are less than perfect, a real person in fact who is keen to understand all of the prospect's business. The prospect's response could be gold, as they smile and mention they were thinking about changing the software before summer. Just write it down.

"Anything missed?" is a gem and over the years has uncovered some nuggets including, "Actually, yes! I'm leaving the business in 2 weeks." Or, "We own the software company." The point is to ask this question and learn everything, the good often very good, the bad, better to know now and sometimes the downright ugly.

Toby has been writing with speed, looks up and says, "So that is it, Sally, I now have my fact find?"

"Oddly enough, Toby, no, not yet! What you have now is a list of question topics that could help you have a wonderful conversation with a prospect and learn plenty - just not enough to sell. Toby scratches his head.
"But I have asked loads and now know, well loads and my notebook is full."
- You do now know lots of information about the prospect's business today. Just not enough to sell, especially if looking to net a big fish that we understand swims slowly.

Toby is scratching his head some more. It happens in training. Time for a demonstration.

On the floor the letters are laid out one under the other on a column, WHATSAS in blue and the column title is Today. I ask someone to be a prospect, the decision maker at a company, any company and I become the salesperson. Jumping in at Step 4, it is role play after all, I ask them What questions then step literally to the How then Area then To Whom, next Special and Anything Missed before Summarising, which is Step 5.

Turning to the room and asking, "Can I sell the prospect anything, do I have gaps, a problem that needs solving or opportunities I could help create?"

Often there is a perplexed "Yes, of course, you sell IT, they have IT so, yes."

Next, the same letters in Pink are laid in a second column on the floor, the column title is Future. I begin again, what is it in your words that you do now and what is it you're looking to do in the future? What is your range now, what are you looking to include in the future? What is your turnover now, what are you looking for your turnover to be in the future? Every today question is followed by a future question.

Looking to the room and asking, "Now, do I have a gap?" Only when you have established a gap can you potentially pitch to fill it? Not that we are pitching yet, there are still questions about how, area, to whom, special and anything missed to ask. Importantly follow by a look into the future. A question that is prefaced with, "Just imagine, two years from now, what will your turnover, margin, and range be?" Their system one brain races to the future. They imagine how it could look and share this with you. Pure gold, you have noted what they are imagining for the future.

We continue the role-play sales call and when a gap is established the gap card goes down on the floor. GAP. Walking through this reinforces the flow, and the format of a conversation. What they strive for in the future, less what they have today is your gap. How they would like the systems to look, less how it looks, is your gap, the area they want to trade in, less where they trade today, is your gap. To whom, or whom they would sell to, less whom they do sell to, is the gap. How they plan to remain special in the future is your gap. There might not be a gap for every question. But asking and understanding everything is important.

Remember, this is a conversation that should flow - today and the future, gap weaved into a call, Zoom or walk around a factory. The more questions you must pull from and the more practice you have using WHATSAS even if just a coffee, the easier the flow will be.

You don't know what you don't know might seem like an odd suggestion when you are at the heart of a need find when you are looking for the gap. Keep in mind that sometimes your prospects might not know exactly what they need, and it is up to you to help them find out. When your prospect, especially a big fish, is happy doing it their way, the way they have always done it, then looking to change can be daunting for them. Changing to a new way could be a slow decision that takes time. Remember, the limbic brain decides, based on like and trust. A big fish prospect might think change is not required or that a problem will resolve itself. Your job is to understand all your prospect's needs, gaps, and problems that need solving and that might require some digging.

Accepting a reply at face value and omitting to understand the reasoning behind it could see you miss a notably bigger opportunity. A sale depends on knowing all your client's needs today and in the future.

Needs can begin small, like one Mac Book today. Then develop into a real problem, like twenty Mac Books by the end of the year. This creates a strong desire for a solution. A big fish's needs develop differently from a small fish's. A small fish's need for one Mac Book is different from looking for a new technology partner. That commitment requires thought and research.

Good salespeople "Dig" out implied needs, they ask about the future and importantly the consequences should the problem not be resolved.

If this is sounding tricky, remember it is part of a conversation, be sincere and curious. You're looking to understand the whole picture not just the transactional need for right now.

When in the habit of using WHATSAS, being thorough and noting all the answers, being confident in asking about the consequences and remembering to let the conversation flow, then you will come away with a clear list of gaps.

Being thorough with WHATSAS will provide a full understanding of the business ambition, and what and how they want to achieve it. Rarely with all the information will you receive objections. Being thorough uncovers everything you need to know at the top of the call. Knowing what they want to achieve and that doing nothing won't achieve their end goal, is a powerful moment.

The final part of WHATSAS is your summary and has a step all of its own, step 5 - The gap.

Wayne and Olly are back. In this story note how they approach steps 4 and 5 of a sales call differently and the resulting outcomes.

Wing it Wayne was a lad, a geezer, a fella who liked the banter, the laughter, and the ladies!

Wing it Wayne flew by the seat of his pants. He'd received real grief about how he messed up a meeting with Bill Fates at Major Manufacturing. Like it was his fault there was traffic! Wayne was secretly chuffed though because today he'd earned an excellent opportunity. Now was the time to reaffirm his status as a brilliant salesperson.

Today, Tuesday, Wayne had an introductory call with a lapsed client who had worked with his company over ten years ago. Wayne had looked at the CRM. Wayne had got lucky, a cold call to Pamela the new PA for Billy Bobs, IT director at AJ Energy and he was in. He'd used his charm offensive with Pamela and the result was an appointment. The pressure was on.

On time, Wayne spent a good ten minutes flirting with Pamela. She was old enough to be his mother but who cared? He was all about creating a good impression. He'd even worn his new aftershave, "One In A Million." He knew he was! Pamela fluffed her hair, smiled at Wayne, and showed him into Billy Bob's office.

Wayne, hands on hips, said, "Hello!" sat down and asked Billy if he was alright. Billy replied "Yes!" Wayne opened his laptop and launched into a detailed presentation about his tech company, beginning with the year they were created, how they had grown, won awards and supported many great clients. He showed how they offered IT support, software, hardware, and cyber security - could run a free dark web check and how their experts were world famous and attended dark web conferences. Wayne even mentioned the very spacious car park!

He took a sip of water and continued talking, about how he knew Billy Bobs 'company's needs and their tech support requirements as he had looked at the file from ten years ago. Wayne was up to speed with their existing tech requirements based on the CRM which he had looked at.

Billy Bobs, the newly appointed IT director, was aghast, his jaw pretty much on the floor. Although his mouth was open, he had said almost nothing, one word in fact. Then Wayne looked to Billy and said, "So we are good to begin working together, then?"

Billy Bob's stood up, baffled and walked out. Pamela, his new PA said Wayne was amazing, that his attention to detail was spot on, that he knew the history of JA Energy, had worked with them before and said they were good. This was anything but good. How could he pitch without knowing anything about the business? It was three times what it was in 2010, employed 50 more people and was operating worldwide.

Wayne had missed out. Back to LinkedIn to source someone who cared about the customer, talked in their language, and looked to see how they could help.

Olly had heard about Wayne's wasted opportunity at Major Manufacturing. A real shame as that was a gift. Olly wondered how Wayne lived without decent commission, recognition, and an annual bonus.

Olly was excited about today. He was back at Maxim Manufacturing to understand what problems they had to solve and what opportunities Maxim was looking to create. Olly was keen to know how his tech company could help them today and most importantly over the next eighteen months.

Elliott, the IT director, was delightful and the Jaffa cakes were a good idea. However, if he were to win the business, first he really needed a detailed understanding of how his company could help.

Sitting down, taking notes, assuming nothing, Olly asked about what Maxim did now, product range, turnovers, budget, margin and what they were looking to achieve in the future. He wanted to know how they used their IT, how they prevented cyber-attack and operated remotely, what worked well and what didn't, what they enjoyed about working with their current IT supplier and what they liked less. Then, how many people tapped into IT and how this would look in 18 months, what area of the UK they were based in, how remote working had played out and how it would look in the future. He also had to understand who used the IT across all departments and how Maxim's customers logged onto their accounts, how technology support was introduced to the teams and who used it daily or less frequently.

All these questions would help Olly to understand how he could help. Elliott gave detailed replies, asking only once why he was interested in future turnover. Olly explained that he wanted to create solutions to help assist the company reach their goals. Elliott was impressed with how thorough the questions were and importantly, when asked if he did nothing to address a vulnerable security software situation, what the consequences would be. That really made him think!

Before summarising, Olly checked if he had missed anything about Maxim that could be relevant. That enabled Elliot to share about his company looking to work with suppliers who had an eye on green energy. They were hoping for government funding and if their supplier could display green credentials they would receive more.

Olly looked up after saying little and noting lots. He summarised that Elliott was keen to be fully safe from cyber-attack, update all hardware so that it could work remotely for his team of 50 and investigate the backup cloud storage. All this was needed within the next 12 months, with cyber safety critical now. Olly reaffirmed that working with like-minded businesses was key, green credentials mattered and that the budget was in place for some this year and some next - £180k in total.

"Wow!" thought Elliott. The detail was captured perfectly by Olly. This chap was good and having agreed that was indeed what he wanted to achieve they diarised for Olly to be back next week with suggested solutions as to how his tech company could solve his IT problems and maybe even create opportunities for his people.

26 Money Talk

Money Talk

Let's talk money because it is, after all, just money.
At the 'What 'part of WHATSAS please ask about margin, turnover, goals, avo (average value order) and targets, please talk money. Money is a wonderful measure. If looking for a long-lasting relationship with an opportunity to celebrate when your future clients achieve what they set out to when deciding to work with you, then understanding the money is a good idea.

Sometimes people squirm at the idea of asking a prospect about money. The perception is that money is a dirty word. This is understandable, as for years money was hushed, not talked about. House prices, for example, no one knew what you paid for yours or what you sold it for, now everything is visible online. Savings and how much or little you had, was a conversation avoided and replaced with weather. Wages, salaries, bonuses, and target achievement were for many years hidden or whispered. The opposite of the Wolf on Wall Street image of dollars everywhere. Leonardo in character shares how money is the oxygen of capitalism, and he wants to breathe more than any man alive.

So, with a backdrop of talking about money in hushed tones or the opposite of shouting about and reveling in it, no wonder money causes a potential stumbling block.

There is most likely a study somewhere to back up how we view money, through our life lens. For example, imagine you are 16, working Saturdays part-time in a cafe and earning £30 including tips most weeks. Then a pair of shoes costing £300 might seem ridiculous, far too much, too expensive. If your job sees you earning a six-figure salary plus expenses and a fabulous company car, then the £300 pair of shoes might seem like a bargain. In business taking off your lens and seeing the price or investment through the eyes of your prospect is key. If you think £30 is a lot of money then when pitching for a hundred times more you might be in awe, disbelieving the value. Move the lens, money is a measure of value you can bring, Time to put your life lens to one side and win business with ease talking big money as you deliver big value!

The good news is that in business, money is an excellent measure. Like weight in kilos, the temperature in Celsius, in business it is money. Companies House don't ask about how your review ratings are, and your accountant is less interested in the brand of coffee you have in the canteen. The measure is money. So be in the habit of talking money, profit margins, return on investment, turnover, targets, commission, average value order (avo) and goals. If you shy away from it, you are likely to miss key information and reassurance that you can be a successful solution provider or opportunity creator for this company.

One great habit around commission in successful companies is targeting on profit or margin. When companies target only on turnover there is an opportunity for salespeople like Wing It Wayne to slash prices and sell cheaply at volume without any notion as to whether it is profitable for a company. Paying commission on turnover to reps who are costing the business money is a bad idea! When sales reps and teams are targeted on profit their commercial understanding accelerates and their ability to negotiate around margin is empowered. Lots of money in the till is only a good thing if it is way more than the money going straight back out.

Back to ROI Return on Investment, a favorite phrase of mine and relevant to sales, training and reading this book.
A return on investment of time and money. If you buy this book for £20, read it and put it in a drawer thinking excellent content,

then do nothing with it, your return on investment of money is mediocre. You read a book; it passed the hours. However, if you take every single module and start using them, practicing, and making them habits, or better still roll it out to the whole company so that they all begin to generate their results from the £20 spent, then your return on investment will be huge and well done!

Return on investment of time is also key and frequently forgotten. If you spend a total of twenty hours reading this book and putting it in a drawer and thinking that was nice, then the return is 20 hours of feeling nice, educated, and informed. If you take it and spend more time sharing the content with others who use it to create their results, then your return on investment of time is massive.

In a sales call, on Step 4 of WHATSAS, asking about money. Turnover now and future forecast, the future matters. Ask about now and future, goals targets, Avo, and margin. Take note. This information will be key to your targeted pitch. Understanding the return, you can bring will boost your confidence and wipe out money objections. Better still when your new prospect is a customer and they achieve the results they wanted, that they brought you in to deliver, then you can celebrate together. If you don't know what they are because you avoided asking, mistake. Talking money ensures you know what they are looking to achieve and being confident when talking money matters!

Remember in Step 1, the plan and prep of a sales call? Understanding that your product or service can deliver a solution or opportunity ensures your belief in bringing a clear return on investment to the prospect. It also matters, when prospecting, that you are spending time with the decision maker and people who look like your ideal prospect to ensure you bring yourself a clear return on investment of your time.

Value matters when talking about money. Knowing the value,

you can bring will see you walk tall, shoulders back, inspiring confidence.

27 Step 5, The Gap

No Gap No Sale

Throughout WHATSAS you listened without 'but' and took notes. You now have a full picture of what the prospect is looking to solve or achieve. You are now armed with facts and figures, the full picture. Now for Step 5, the last S in WHATSAS and your summary.

Step 5 is, "The Gap." and worth remembering, "No Gap, no sale." People buy to solve problems or to create opportunities. The buying motives are at play but without clearly defined gaps you will have nothing specific to pitch to.

When summarising the gaps be careful not to go back over the whole hour or more conversation that you had when you were fact-finding. Summarise only the gaps, in their language. "So, you're looking to accelerate growth within the next twelve months! Updating the IT infrastructure is a key part of this and importantly, working with a supplier who values reducing the carbon footprint."

Step 5 is short and sweet and underlines, as well as highlights, what problems you will look to solve or what opportunities will be created. Step 5 is the foundation for your pitch. Make your gap easy to understand, in their language and make sure they agree.

Seeking their agreement at the end with a simple, "Is that correct?" leads you beautifully into Step 6 - your pitch. With big fish, this can happen weeks later in a separate call.
You might suggest that you will take all the details and be back with creative solutions that will provide exactly what they need to fill those gaps. In this case, to help provide growth, support IT and reduce carbon footprint. You flagged, in signposting that you would be back. Do not leave this call without your pitch or

presentation date booked and agreed upon.

If you walk away now without further commitment you leave the door wide open for a competitor to sweep in before you.

28 Step 6, About The Pitch

It's Not About You!

Really, it's not about you, ever! The reason you are in front of a prospect with an opportunity to sell them something is either because they have a problem to solve, or you can help them to create an opportunity.

In Step 4 WHATSAS you spent time understanding the problems to solve and opportunities you can help with. Then in Step 5 you neatly summarised what they were.

Excellent! Now on to Step 6 of the selling process, your pitch, sales story, or as it is sometimes referred to, Adding to Knowledge. This is your opportunity to share how you and your company can help make their life simply brilliant.

Sales reps often jump right in and begin with the pitch, usually a very long pitch, oh dear! The pitch is best delivered succinctly and should be specific to the prospect's needs, in their language.

Toby looks up, "I have a great pitch, Sally! I take in a presentation and begin talking them through it slide by slide until we reach page 34 the carpark!"

If only Toby was joking! In the 1980s, Exchange and Mart created superb-looking presentations that the reps could take out to show their clients. They were chunky, foam filled, their black plastic covers packed with many glossy pages, slick, on brand and a full history lesson about the company. The detail inside was powerful and shared how many people would see your advert. There were pictures that showcased each region, the reader, the business, the scale, the design. Shall I go on? In the 1980s a full-on all-out pitch and presentation lasting hours was a thing. Now, we live in a world where we consume information at such a speed, we get bored if a video is over two minutes or a report is more than a page. In a world where getting to the point quickly and speed are normal, bringing out a presentation to launch into a full history lesson is a huge turnoff.

Toby looks up puzzled. "But we need to know the detail." Absolutely *you* need to know the detail of your product and service, *you* need to understand the important elements, the process, and the results. The data, stats and how it all works are powerful tools in your toolbox. Negating understanding the detail of your product or service is a bad idea.

Your pitch however, needs to be conversational and address the specifics that were summarised in Step 5. It should include differentiators and talk in a language that your prospects relate to. It should talk about other companies who look just like your prospects, what you did for them and the results they achieved. Sharing from a testimonial, third-party viewpoint is way more powerful than talking at them.

Remember the story about the coffee shop and Lucy the owner saying her coffee and cake are fab? Also, Tom, is a frequent visitor to Lucy's coffee shop saying the coffee and cake are fab. We trust Tom over Lucy because he is impartial and has no bias towards saying how great the coffee and cake are. If you can remember this when you pitch and talk about what you do from a third-person perspective, you are onto a winner because you will be trusted. Limbic brain!

The pitch is bringing solutions, and this is the time you need your prospect's limbic brain in your corner, liking and trusting you. When we decide to buy, this is emotional. In training, to reinforce the message, a slide shows a man looking dishevelled, having just rolled out of bed, not pretty, nor glamorous and not attractive. The next picture shows a kitchen, messy with stuff all over, the washing up bottle on the side and a shelf or drawer with stuff that just gets put on it. The slide shows a shabby car, dirty and could use a wash, has shoes left inside and dog hair, crisp packets, and empty bottles of water. The final picture shows a lady at a gym. She is working out, sweating, and carrying a few extra pounds. All these pictures are reality and most normal. When we wake up, we always look less than brilliant, kitchens have stuff in, cars have mess and startlingly when working out, we sweat! This is reality and yet for some bizarre reason, as a nation, we tend not to want to buy reality. We want to buy the feeling. That old limbic brain again!

Big brands play on this beautifully. A teenager's ambition is to own a Michael Kors bag, Nike trainers or an Apple watch all because of how they think it will make them feel. Ironically, thanks to product adaptation the feeling is short-lived.

Back to the Feeling. The next slide shows the perfect kitchen in a perfect showroom. Not a stuff shelf in sight, no washing up liquid on the side, and a fake fruit bowl placed at a certain angle. The designer brand hand wash signals a fabulous life that feels great if we buy this high gloss, super exclusive, perfectly tidy kitchen! The picture of David Gandy modelling Autograph at M&S most likely sells more than an out-of-shape fat chap. The suggestion is that if we buy David Gandy's range of clothes then we will feel good. No wonder celebrities endorse brands, watches, and clothes! We associate a feeling with the celeb that passes to the brand. It makes us feel good. Remember the Lynx adverts? Spray this and you all become attractive! The new cars that we take for a test drive have been valeted and there is absolutely no dust inside or out, no scuffs or dog hair; they are immaculate and smell wonderful. Just one of the many reasons we buy a new car is for the smell. We imagine how we will feel if we have this car in our life, on the drive. It is all about feeling. Historically in January, as a nation, we rush to sign up for gym membership, often more than £1000 to make us feel better. As we hand over the cash, we feel that we have done something positive towards becoming healthy, overlooking the fact that a class has not yet been tried. Why do we hand over money for a membership we are unlikely to use? We do it because we saw an image of a stunning lady or gentleman working out, their body shape and physique perfect, exactly how you want yours to be. They glow and do not sweat or look uncomfortable. All of this before we talk about airbrushing and dive deep into advertising.

If the feeling was not part of the reason we buy and had no impact whatsoever on our choice of product or service, imagine! We would be driven by price or speed. We would mostly likely all go to Asda for a jumper, Dacia for a car and buy Savers brands at the supermarket - after all, without feeling it's just food!

Toby has a question. "I thought pitching was all about features and benefits?"
- Great point Toby! For many years courses would see you make lists on the left of the facts, products, or services you sold, then on the right-hand column, you would flip it into the benefit delivered by having the product or service in your life. It absolutely has a place, but it is not **why** we buy because that is emotional, based on how people feel. How do your clients feel about you, do they love you, like you, rave about you, and enjoy the experience of working with you?

Toby sits and asks, "So, we need to get in touch with our feelings to sell?"
- **Yes**, Toby, absolutely **yes**!

Let's look at some organisations that do this brilliantly without you even noticing. Take Virgin Atlantic, the prestigious airline. When you buy a holiday with Virgin you don't just buy a hotel room and a flight, you become a VIP. Virgin treats you and address you as a VIP, a very important person. You become a VIP for booking your holiday with them and you feel great. When purchasing Marks and Spencer's food, especially the dine-in range for a special occasion, you don't buy any food, you buy M&S food, and you feel fabulous. John Lewis is master at this. Remember their Christmas adverts from the past few years? Of course, you do. The monster under the bed, Moshi! The Man on the Moon featuring Elton John, the alien lighting up Christmas. The dragon one is a favourite. It takes you on an emotional journey, meets a cute dragon, the dragon is lonely to begin with then finds a friend, how sweet. Next, the dragon laughs and breathes fire setting everything alight, oh dear! The cute dragon is back, lonely again, how sad. Then on Christmas Day when the villagers are served with Christmas pudding, it is cold, and the brandy needs to be flamed. Bring on the cute dragon who saves Christmas dinner, well shall we say saves Christmas! Throughout this advert your emotions, how you feel, are up, down, back up and delighted with a happy ending. Odd, as John Lewis doesn't sell you anything. No pictures of socks, sprays of perfume or blast of a hairdryer, nothing. John Lewis recognise that if we feel positive towards them, their store and their brand in relation to Christmas, then it is their online or high street store we will shop at.

It is all about feeling. The last example is the most powerful and, in some measure, scary. Think McDonald's, one of the world's biggest, fast-food outlets. Remember when Covid restrictions were lifted, and cars queued for miles to buy a burger from a McDonald's drive-through? McDonald's is brilliant at understanding and tapping into the impact of emotion when purchasing. Every time we buy anything the big M and the "I'm Lovin 'it!" jingle are front of mind. Wow! Take a minute, you just bought Mc Nuggets, a cheeseburger and salty chips and you're "Loving" it! Love is the most precious emotion of all, saved for family, partners, and friends, now placed in the same context as a 99p cheeseburger! Really? It gets worse or arguably better. To cheer up our children we think that giving them a "Happy Meal" will make them feel happy. Whether talking about nutritional benefits or not, one thing I know to be true is that sustained happiness is rarely found in chips, nuggets, and a full-fat coke! Suggestions to children and families that kids can be happy if they eat junk food is misleading and as much as I find this marketing uncomfortable, I also applaud it. Other businesses could learn from McDonald's. Do you share how your customers love working with you, how they like what you do, how they value you and that you feel like a part of their team? Maybe you're too shy, it seems boastful and a bit gushy, this whole feeling thing.

Simply put, if a hamburger can be associated with love, a meal in a box supposedly makes us happy, and if retailers tell us emotional stories and an airline calls us VIPS, then how good are we at talking about feeling in our business?

The critical piece of information to understand when pitching is that people buy feelings, and how it makes you feel is based on like and trust.

Toby looks exasperated and states, "So my long presentation pitch needs to go, features and benefits are outdated, and I need to get into feelings?"

- In a nutshell Toby, yes, if you want to sell more and have happier customers. If in any doubt that feelings determine purchase, I wonder if you recall the high street jewellers, Ratners?

Back in the 1980s, Ratners was a well-known, highly successful High Street jewellery chain. With a store in most towns and cities, they sold jewellery that was pretty, looked good and was a fabulous price. The team at Ratners had found a way to make gold jewellery look stunning yet weigh less, making the price to the consumer readily attainable. Zirconia in a hollow gold band could pass to the untrained eye as a diamond and gold ring. Their sales soared until the 23rd of April 1991!

Gerald Ratner, the owner, was at a posh, black-tie charity event. He was asked how he could afford to sell their jewellery so cheaply and his immediate reply was, "Because it's absolute **crap**!"

The next day the tabloid newspapers featured Gerald Ratner on every front page with a speech bubble or headline, "Our jewellery is absolute crap." The news carried, magazines and press featured pictures of Gerald, his stores, and his crap jewellery. Overnight, sales in all the stores plummeted. The stores stayed the same, same staff, product range and prices, in fact, everything was the same. What changed was our feeling towards it. As a consumer, we did not want to feel that were buying crap, jewellery. This is an excellent example of negating to see the value in how your customers and prospects feel about you, in this case, a change in feelings towards Ratners was a disaster.

Feelings matter when pitching and so does the language you use. Most companies 'salespeople launch into talking about themselves. They begin with we do, our people, I am or the company does. When a pitch, sales story, presentation or adding to knowledge begins with "We do, we are, we make, we provide, our people," the prospect thinks, "So what?" Instead, you could ignite their brain by sharing a story about other companies who look just like them, the pains you removed and the results you delivered. You could do this if you are in tune with what your customers say about you.

When you share success stories about similar-looking businesses and people, the prospect's system one brain stays with you, engaged and listening. You are sharing a relatable story and building trust. Launch into a pitch or full-out presentation that is self-focused, too long, and dull and you turn the prospect off. Talking about you is dull but talking about them is interesting! Ever had one of those people in your network who make every conversation about themself, turns your moment to be about them, and makes each topic somehow about them? You know that person, we have all met them. Inside, we shut down, glaze over and disengage. Sharing a pitch is the same, make it about them and win the business!

Sometimes sales reps wing the pitch and have no clue what a sales story is. They prefer to email a pdf document, refer to the brochure or website and then expect a "Yes"! At best they might pull out a back-dated PowerPoint that showcases the company history, nice pictures about, you guessed it their company HQ, canteen, and carpark. The PowerPoint is standard, the same as every other company trying to sell what you sell. A generic, dull PowerPoint that looks like every other is not going to entice a 'Yes 'anytime soon. Excellent salespeople understand that standing out and being different is a great way to ignite your prospect's brain and win business. Are you saying the same as everybody else? Practising, rehearsing or even investing in creating a specific pitch is viewed as a silly idea. Why would they, they are far too busy as they've not hit the target yet and so they engage Wing It Wayne's approach and, well, wing it! The PowerPoint might include a bar chart, snazzy slide or data and often lists the many awards they have won at all the events they sponsored. The neocortex part of your prospect's brain, if still engaged, will be excited, it loves facts and figures. Remember from an earlier chapter, it is hugely flawed. Unable to decide regardless of the size or credibility of the award, however, detailed the data or impressive the bar chart. The limbic brain makes decisions on, "Do I like and trust right now, with an outdated, unoriginal PowerPoint and sloppy, unprofessional pitch?" The answer is, "No!"

Years ago, a cool business leader asked what I thought of his company's new video and web content. He is a trusted friend, a highflyer in fact and as such deserved an honest reply. The style of video and content, the look of the website and its design were superb, but the language was self-focused. The new website and video had been created to entice new prospects to get in touch, and to build trust. It talked only about what the business did, we do, our people. It was all about them and told from their perspective. The opportunity to build trust by sharing how their customers viewed them was missed. To build trust with a wider audience it could have showcased the company's success by using language or images from their customers about how it helped them. It could have shared stories in testimonial style that new prospects could relate to and importantly could trust because they were relatable. Back to Tom and Lucy in the coffee shop and who we trust more.

The cool business leader went on to highlight every time we, I or the company name was mentioned and flipped it into testimonial style language helped by using transitional phrases. The same exercise with a large accountancy firm saw them remove the team photo from the home page and replace it with a scroller banner, a variety of existing happy clients. Now when looking at their website, as a prospect, the first thing you see is a company that looks like you and was experiencing the same problems you now have. Next, you read how this accounting firm helped them and the results that were achieved. Trusted testimonials on a home page sharing what you do but from your customers 'viewpoint! It worked and enquiry numbers increased.

Wing It Wayne and Rex demonstrated beautifully that the show-up and throw-up, firing data, statistics, and marketing referring to an outdated generic pdf or flyer simply does not work. To win new business, upsell and cross-sell you need to stand out, share how others feel and be specific to the prospect's needs, not excited to shout about you.

Your pitch, whether face-to-face, on a call or online, needs to lead with the prospect's issues. Lead with the pains or problems they want to solve, the opportunities and results they are looking to achieve, and then they will be listening with you and engaged. Your pitch, sales story or adding to knowledge needs to be focused on what matters to them and stand out for the right reasons.

Do you know your USP, the unique reasons people buy from you? Do you really know what you can bring that others cannot? Do you know and share what makes you different, your differentiators?

About six years ago I took a call from a senior partner in a prestigious, wealth management firm. The request was about whether I offered negotiation training. The team of recruits were struggling to secure the deal, secure business and win new accounts. The flaw that the senior team had identified was a lack of negotiation skills.

Listening to further examples of accounts drifting away and after talking with the new recruits, it was clear that negotiation was not the problem. Negotiation rarely began because as soon as fees were mentioned, they began to stumble, stutter, or even sweat! There was little, if any understanding of the firm's key differentiators in comparison to other wealth management firms. The new team members thought their fees were excessive, notably greater than the industry standards. They also thought their fees were high in comparison to their earnings and the lens they were looking through was their own. (See Money Talk chapter).

Speaking with the team it was clear that if they understood why the firm charged what they did, the years of expertise, the links with the Bank of England, the reputation of investment in super successful startups and that when clients began working with them they stayed for years and referred; if the newer team understood the value they brought and believed in it, then asking for the fee would be easy. They did not understand and so when the price was mentioned, they squirmed, were not confident and withdrew from the conversation. No wonder accounts were not won!

If you want to own your superior price, you need a sensational story and that means knowing and owning your differentiators. Only then can you share reasons why your customers pay more so that you can articulate the value and own it. Shoulders back, walk tall, show confidence, and know your worth!

29 Step 6a, Create A Pitch

The story below showcases how Wayne got it very wrong when pitching, unlike Olly, can you see why?

Wing it Wayne was a lad, a geezer, a fella who liked the banter, the laughter and the ladies!

Wing it Wayne had been called at the last minute to pitch to Morris Booth. They were a new enquiry that had gone to Dan, but as Dan was off with Covid and everyone else was busy, Wayne had been called on to pitch.

Wayne was cool with this because he knew how to pitch. He began to print out a 38-page document from back in the day when he pitched far more often. With approx 600 words a page, it was a full document. Packed with data, facts, figures and bar charts. It began with the company history, starting in the late 1970s and continued across five slides to today, 2021 with the new office layout. It even had a picture of the up-to-date modern reception area with the fish tank.

The slides covered every facet of the business, tech support, cyber support, hardware, software and every other kind of support. The help desk had a page, the engineers their own page, and there was even a Meet the Leadership Team page with detailed biographies and the reps 'page.

This was going to take some time!

Armed with a copy for each member of The Morris & Booth team, Wayne arrived on time and this time he remembered to wear a tie.

Before sitting down, Wayne hooked up the projector and began on slide 1. An hour in, he was aware of some fidgeting, yawning and shuffling. Odd, as he was only sharing the photocopier

Christmas party story and that was funny! Another half hour and the yawns were no longer stifled when two of the four excused themselves. Then a PA came in asking for the other two guys and access to the room for the next appointment. Wayne was sure it was a rescue call. He was left with 38 slides still to go and nobody to present to. At least they all had a hard copy, thought Wayne.

He packed up and headed back to the office. He had omitted to look at the CRM that detailed the gaps, the solutions required and the budget for Morris Booth. Wayne knew how to pitch!

Oddly, this company never contacted him or his tech support company again. He heard on the grapevine that they went to work with a competitor. How rude, that presentation took hours to print and five ink cartridges!

Olly was nicknamed **On It Olly** for good reason. When it came to the pitch he was definitely on it! He was always pitching, answering the phone, posting on LinkedIn, writing an email or making a call. He would be talking in the customer's language about how diligent IT directors always turned to him for solutions; how Financial Directors needing value and security used Olly because his managed service delivered results and was on budget; about the frustrated company owner who called him because he needed his online shop to work and how he was fed up of being fobbed off by his current tech support company. Talking in the third person, the testimonial style was Olly's second language.

Olly recognised he needed to impress, to stand out, to own his price and that meant understanding his company's differentiators and using them. Being mediocre and stating that they gave good service and had a car park was dull, a yawn and expected anyway. Stating that his company was consistently winning awards, that when customers began using him, they stayed, referred and that if on occasion they left, they came back. He referred to how his customers viewed him as an extension of their team, they trusted him and enjoyed working with the expert cybersecurity people who supported him. Olly shared how his company continued to grow in an ever-competitive marketplace because they delivered results, achieved the newest software solutions and kept companies protected wherever they were. That is why Olly was frequently referred and he was happy to share this fact.

When Olly met Elliot (with more Jaffa cakes), it was more conversational than a full-on, old-school 1980's, A4 ring binder pitch. Olly had a document already prepared on his laptop that contained all the relevant detail. This would be looked at and emailed post-call. The pitch however was conversation. Olly shared with passion how his IT company was proud to support businesses that shared the same problems as Elliott's. How his team diagnosed exactly what IT was required and in a matter of months the hardware could be updated, storage put on the cloud and his clients slept soundly. He shared how working to budget and an accurate time scale delighted IT directors just like Elliott. Projects ran to schedule and stayed on budget. The 24-hour help desk kicked in from day one and creating a cyber-safe environment was a priority. Olly told Elliott that his company was ready to roll on his say-so, that they wanted to work with him and felt it was a good fit. Other companies had been super impressed by the delivery speed, efficiency and professional approach of the engineers as they worked with companies to make every new IT innovation happen safely and with ease. Frequently, the clear communication right through the rollout was praised.

Elliott smiled when Olly talked about how his company was also focusing on green credentials, in the way they recycled old hardware, reduced mileage by using Zoom calls and were upgrading their fleet to electric. They even won awards for green innovation in 2021.

Elliott continued to smile when asked how he was feeling about everything. All Elliott needed to confirm was the terms and he was good to go.

"Wow!" thought Elliott. "Olly and his company are exactly the right fit for us.

Standout for the right reasons!

Baking is not my "go-to" pastime, but if I did ever need to make a cake, biscuits or some cheese straws then the first point of reference would be a cookery book.

It is the same when creating your pitch. We understand that pitches should be specific to the prospect's needs, talking about problems you can solve and solutions you can bring, all from a third-party perspective. Each conversational pitch will be different. Some want cake, others a biscuit and some a cheese straw.

Toby looks up and says, "So, we need to have a recipe book packed full of different pitches?"
- Almost Toby! You do need a recipe book, or as Mike Weinberg calls it a Power Statement. You need a document that notes what you do, just one line; all the problems you solve, solutions you bring, opportunities you create and growth achieved written from a testimonial perspective. Then what you do, short, sweet and easy to understand and lastly a long and fabulous list of your differentiators.

Toby sighs, "Sally, this will take ages." Toby is right! Done well, it takes a team a good few hours to work on. When those hours have produced your first draft it will most likely change and be periodically updated as you note more problems solved and more results achieved. The document you are creating is a living document, your "go-to" recipe book and investing time in making it will save a massive amount of time in the future and help your pitch.

The great news is that when your Power Statement is complete it can be used by the whole company. Marketing can refer to it when creating campaigns. If going networking with MDs and Business leaders, the new reps can refer to the phrase that talks about how MDs and Business leaders looking for IT Solutions have you on speed dial. Account managers looking to influence sales can talk about other clients who created results using new IT solutions. Reception can share how customers enjoy visiting your headquarters because they feel like a part of the family.

Before posting on social media, referring to a power statement can see a post begin through the eyes of your prospect and receive greater engagement. When at an exhibition and asked what you do, your default reply will always be third-party rather than 'I do 'or 'I am'. In team meetings sharing success from the customer's viewpoint will lock in the style of language. Cold, warm or hot calls, your website or any touchpoint - when you share stories from a customer's viewpoint you're winning!

When a whole company is in the habit of talking about the business from a third-party perspective the results are transformational. Trust is built through language and then sales soar. Remember the limbic brain?

Next, create your Power Statement! In training, ahead of any talk about pitching, the task is to write a line about what you do, a total of ten problems you solve, pains you remove, opportunities you create and results achieved. Ten is a good beginning but remember this list will grow. Next comes your offering followed by at least five of your differentiators. On It, Olly's example below will help in this task.

Olly's List

Problems Solved by Tech Technology
- Ageing software
- Vulnerable data
- Laptops and hardware are old and unreliable
- Staff try to sort tech issues
- Support phone line engaged or rings out
- Worried about keeping data safe
- Different tech suppliers for email, CRM and phones
- Worried about cyber attacks and ransomware
- Lack of resources in the business to roll out big IT change
- How we keep staff vigilant around cyber crime and phishing emails
- Old servers
- No password protection
- Struggle to keep licences renewed and fit for purpose
- The phone system is old
- Teams meetings won't work on existing hardware
- Insurance premiums skyrocketed

Tech Technology Differentiators
- Different tech offerings to other tech companies
- Fully managed IT that surpasses the industry standard
- Deliver peace of mind
- Call any day, 365 days a year
- Sensational, expert team, partners and engineers
- World-class partners
- Our clients love working with us and stay with us
- Our clients refer us

If this task is proving tricky, refer to reviews or recommendations your customers have left. Better still, ask them. Time to get familiar with the value you bring and to own it with confidence.

Once your first draft is complete, share it within the company and look to update and include new shared success stories.

Then print it. To make it a habit that becomes a new language it needs to live. Include it in meetings, 121s, and post it on walls and in presentations. Do whatever it takes to ensure that all your company shares elements of your Power Statement. This document, just like a recipe book, would never be used as a whole; you take the bits you need when you need them. Take the recipe specific to what you want to bake, using a transitional phrase or differentiator specific to your prospect's gaps. On It Olly's first power statement is below, it continues to be updated and referred to, importantly it is a key part of his sales process.Next, to the pitch! In training the gaps found using WHATSAS are key. Weave your pitch or sales story around these gaps using elements of your power statements. Remember to make it conversational, and specific to them. Share stories about people who used to have their problems and how you solved them. Be excited and passionate when sharing your differentiators. Displaying passion, enthusiasm and absolute belief will lead you nicely to step 7 - your trial close.

Tech Technology Power Statement - On It Olly, Internal document

1. <u>Headline – Simple, direct and clear</u>

Tech Technology is an extraordinary, liked and trusted IT Managed Service Provider. We work with technology-conscious IT executives in organisations across all sectors to deliver effective, innovative IT solutions, ongoing support and cyber resilience.

2. <u>Note problems solved and results achieved from a third-person perspective. Lead with the customer and share how you help.</u>

IT Directors look to Tech Technology when ageing software is putting their business at risk; when Data is vulnerable, laptops and hardware are not performing and staff are taking way too much time trying to sort things out, all because the helpline is usually engaged.

IT Directors looking for a trusted tech partner to help solve problems and create solutions that would keep their organisation safe and efficient, know to call us.

Tech Managers are frustrated that their poor tech performance is in part due to a mismatch of unreliable IT providers, who know to use Tech Technology to bring it all together.

When Tech Managers have no confidence in their backup or data storage and worry constantly about being compromised by a cyber-attack, that is when they contact Olly to roll out the change.

HR teams tasked with training the whole company on cyber resilience know to turn to Tech Technology for an easy rollout and to avoid being the next news headline.

Newly appointed IT Managers value close links with the expert team at Tech Technology. They are happy that they look at every aspect of tech within the organisation, create tailored solutions and roll out an extensive change programme.

IT Directors who work with Tech Technology sleep well knowing the tech part of their business is taken care of, worrying now a thing of the past.

In recent years enquiries about cyber security have dramatically increased. Business Owners often contact Tech Technology concerned by the increasing threat of a cyber attack and what to do if a ransomware demand is received.

IT Managers who understand that system backups and data storage are critical but need help, call us to update and replace old, hard-to-access servers.

Diligent MDs, who have previously experienced cyber-attack

and now find their teams all used the same password, "Bob123" bring Tech Technology in to educate and help keep the company protected with ongoing training.

Business owners know to turn to Tech Technology for world-class security assessment, advice and solutions on firewalls and secure wifi, training and simply to be protected every day of the year, similar to a concierge service.

Financial Directors looking to feel safe knowing storage is compliant, data protected, and insurance premiums reduced, enjoy working with Tech Technology.

Local firms reach out to Tech Technology as they often don't have all the skills or knowledge in-house. They are looking to save money, consolidate suppliers and work with a trusted partner to advise, create tech solutions and train the team.

Innovation Leaders looking to enhance the communication experience for their customers on call, video and Teams, trust Tech Technology to deliver the finest platforms.

Offering - what you do, keep it simple.

Tech Technology provides award-winning IT services, cloud, comms and cyber, backed by a world-class and highly experienced team to support large and small organisations and keep them safe. We are a forward-thinking business with longstanding customers that trust and rely on our technology expertise. Our engineers across the world help private & public sector organisations and Tech Technology's dedicated team work closely with clients, listening, creating solutions and delivering.

Differentiators - Why you are better, your time to own it, be compelling and standout

Tech Technology continues to grow in a competitive tech market because the offering is very different to other tech companies. We deliver a fully managed IT service using the best technology that surpasses the industry standard.

Tech Technology delivers peace of mind that your business technology is surpassing expectations and that your data is backed up, secure and cared for by the people that know you, and your technology and understand your business.

No one delivers tech support or managed service and looks after their clients with as much passion and enthusiasm, 365 days a year as Tech Technologies people do.

Supporting your business to achieve growth, knowing you are safe, efficient and protected is their speciality. We have without question the most sensational expert team, partners and engineers.

Our relationships with world-class partners allow us to bring unique, tailored solutions to all business and market sectors.

Our clients enjoy the relationship they have with Tech Technology. They say that it feels like they are part of their team, in their corner.

Tech Technology clients, some of twenty years, don't leave us. They value the tech solutions Olly brings and frequently refer to Olly and Tech Technology.

30 Step 7, The Trial Close

What objections?

Step 7 of the sales process is a favourite! It is small, discreet and super powerful. If omitted you open the sale up to a barrage of potential objections, but when you deliver a trial close you are firing on all cylinders, providing you listen without 'but 'for the answer.

The trial close is the litmus test in selling. It shows you where your buyer is in their buying cycle. After brilliant planning and preparation, wonderful intro and empathy followed by signposting where you mention commitment. Then the WHATSAS provided the gaps and your conversational pitch that was passionate and specific to them. Now is the moment, not to close, as many would think, but to trial close.

Ask, "How do you feel about what we have spoken of so far?"

Toby looks up startled, "Is that it, a whole step in just a few words?"

- Yes, Toby, that is it! Just imagine if you missed the trial close and jumped to step 9, the close. If there is any little detail missed, a doubt, a fear or concern, it can easily lead to a "No". How awful would that be, after everything you have covered in steps 1-6? Including a trial close ensures all those niggles, queries or fears are talked about openly without any pressure to make a decision. The system one brain is not looking to run, it's simply answering a question.

Your pitch ends with step 7, "So, how are you feeling about what we have spoken of?" The reply will be one of three.

1. "Absolutely love the suggestion, let's go!" Excellent news but

before displaying a mini fist pump and screaming with delight, chill because Step 8 is next.

2. "Maybe, I'm still unsure about the delivery, roll out or detail." This is your moment to take note and revisit that part of the pitch before checking for new clarity.

3. "No, no way, absolutely not!" If met with this response something has gone very wrong. Revisit your steps and check which step was something missed. By now you should know the gaps and have pitched specifically to them, built rapport and signposted, sharing that the call would be looking for a commitment. Now you are entitled to ask a direct open question. "What happens if you do nothing? How will you achieve the growth, IT solution or remove the pain?"

Once your trial close is complete and the prospect is happy, you can move on to step 8 - your recommendation.

31 Step 8, Recommend

The Advocaat moment

Your prospect has agreed that they like what your pitch suggested and the trial close confirmed they are good to go. Excellent! Now for Advocaat.

Have you ever tasted Advocaat? It's a drink made with eggs, sugar and brandy and tastes a little like custard. When this alcoholic drink is added to lemonade it is referred to as a snowball. It's a drink usually consumed around Christmas and for the record, I am not a fan.

Toby is fidgeting and asks, "What has this yellow drink got to do with step 8?"

A story about Advocaat demonstrates step 8 beautifully.

About six years ago, on a Friday evening after a very busy week, I was ready for a glass of red, preferably a smooth Malbec. Heading to my local supermarket, specifically to the wine aisle, I was amazed to find that there was no red wine - at 7 pm on a Friday! Thinking that maybe white would do, I turned around but there was no white wine on any of the shelves. Perplexed but still in need of a drink, the decision had to be ale. So, embracing my inner Yorkshire lass I decided to buy some Black Sheep. There was no Black Sheep! There was no ale at all. The final thought was that if needs must - and there was a need - then vodka and diet coke would have to do. It was gone at 7 pm, I needed a drink, so headed to the next aisle where there was nothing, no spirits absolutely no alcoholic drinks at this supermarket on a Friday night. Well, not quite true, there was one drink, and it was Advocaat. I had no intention of drinking Advocaat.

In training, turning to the group after telling this story and asking them, "What should I do? What would they do?" They quickly laugh and reply "Go elsewhere, of course!"

They are absolutely correct because you would go elsewhere. Funny then, when we get to the recommendation part of a sale, we often recommend a choice of one. Or put another way, we ask our prospect to go elsewhere for a comparison.

I remember delivering this story in a presentation years ago. Sharing how, when looking to add an extension to our house we set out to get three quotes. Maybe, if the builder had provided three options, then we might have stayed with him. A business leader in the audience had a lightbulb moment. His reputable company provided commercial electrical fit-out to companies. From that day he changed how they quoted. No more one option but a choice of three. The fabulous cable and switches with gold leaf, the mid-range, a popular choice, or if the price was the driver, the value range did the job beautifully. The company's quote-to-sale conversion went up.

As human beings, we like choice, 123, ABC, bronze, silver or gold. Providing choice sees the decision about which one rather than whether to use you or not. People like the autonomy of choosing.

How you wrap up your recommendation is specific to your industry, but taking time to create packages, options or plans will serve you well.

Then, when delivering your options, keep in mind the buying motive of your prospect - pride, profit or fear. Be sure to paint pictures to which your prospect will relate. If pride is a driver, share how the solution is the best, finest most exclusive; if price, talk about value, and return on investment; if fear, then the speed of impact, turnaround and delivery.

When you recommend with passion and conviction, paint pictures of how all the solutions could look and make the prospect feel the importance of these, then you are stepping closer to a "Yes".

32 Step 9, Close

Just ask!

Step 9 of the selling process is the close. This is the bit you have been waiting for, the grand finale of the steps so far and you are ready!

It funny then that many sales are lost because salespeople simply do not ask for the business. According to Zig Ziglar, 63% of salespeople don't ask! The fear of "No" kicks in. What happens if they reject me after all this? You desperately want a "Yes" and yet the ego gets in the way of asking.

Just ask! Ask and you will receive. Don't ask and well, you know the answer to that.

The fear of "No" is a real thing and following the steps of the sale should alleviate it. Back at step 1, the plan and preparation, you believed you could deliver a clear return for the prospect. Your cheese delivered in step 2 assumed you would get this sale. Building rapport and signposting led you nicely to establish the gaps using WHATSAS and your pitch was specific to the gap. The trial close step 7 removed any potential barriers and ironed out any niggles and so you passionately recommended step 8 and painted pictures relating to the buying motive. The end is near, so nearly done, time to ask.

Which close to use, there are so many. Students have created dissertations and essays covering many pages about the many types of close. Let's keep this simple! My favourites are the assumptive close, which you delivered in your cheese or the alternative close.

Assumptive - Shall we begin in February?
Alternative - Which option shall we go with? Silver or gold, 1 or 2, a or b?

The most important part, having delivered your close is sshhhh, not a peep, word or murmur. Play with a pen, and make notes but say *absolutely nothing*. The first person to talk next will lose and if it is you the sale is gone.

Sales reps, usually rookies who have not followed the process thoroughly, may begin to talk, stumble over their words, ask for a decision and then fill the void with clutter, discount and added value or a further reduction. Once you have asked - SHUT UP!

I have sat in situations when staying silent seems to take an age. It's OK, so hold your nerve. It will happen!

There is a real thing that happens when you are over thirty and it gets steadily worse or longer the older you get. Time to gather your thoughts is needed. So, be patient with your prospect. Speedy decisions are rare, especially when a big yes. So, I like and trust you and if a small purchase then maybe a yes is speedier. When faced with a proposition that requires investment, then allow your prospect time to gather their thoughts. They are not thinking no, they are just thinking. Your being quiet enables them to do this but filling the void with noise and words is unhelpful and could lead to a no.

Ask, be quiet and you will receive!

The story below showcases how Wayne got it very wrong closing the sale, unlike Olly, can you see why?

Wing it Wayne's pitch to Morris Booth Ltd was a disaster. The board had all left the room before he'd finished, that was a first. Wing It Wayne was very much in the last chance saloon.

Today, Wednesday, Wayne was feeling smug. His boss mentioned something about a last chance and he had been asked to go and wrap up the Glass House deal. It had taken his company twelve months to even win the opportunity to be in front of Glass House and Mr Glass was known for being tricky.

His boss JB had found an "in", learned about the problems that needed solving and been back to pitch. When JB asked how they were feeling, Mr Glass said it was all good and asked if it would be all right to come back in a day or two and run through the options with him. As it was a big fish, JB agreed and came away.

All Wayne needed to do was wrap it up. Unfortunately, JB was ill so was stuck at home catching up on Peppa Pig with his three-year-old daughter. Wayne was ready, this was his moment, he could hear the bells ringing out in celebration!

Wayne was ushered into Mr Glass's office. He sat down. Mr Glass looked at him and said, "Well?". Wayne looked back and said, "Yes, thank you."

Wayne pulled out the ring binder ready to talk about his tech company's fish tank. Mr Glass asked about his options. Wayne replied that he certainly did have options. Mr Glass asked, "Well, what are they?" Wayne asked," What did he want?"

Mr Glass replied, "You know what I want, your colleague, JB was creating options for me, some ideas so that we could work together."

Wayne agreed. "Yes, he was and yes we could work together."

Wayne sat fidgeting. This was embarrassing. Then Wayne felt a full-on sweat as he suddenly realised that all these suggestions and the proposal were in the CRM. The CRM was at his office, on his desk, something that he rarely looked at, let alone used. The proposal with suggestions was twenty miles away. "Blast!" thought Wayne.

He shuffled in his chair, talked about his company, and filled the space and silence with info about cloud software. Not knowing what he was asking for, he did not bother to ask for anything, just talked about clouds and fish tanks. He wanted to be out of there.

Eventually, he said, "So will you be working with us then?" Mr Glass said nothing and just stared at him. Where was JB? Up until now, he had been ready to go. This Wayne chap was terrible!

Wayne replied, "That will be a "No" then?" and ran out of the office to his car. He was glad that was over but now what? How could he tell JB that he blew it, really blew it? The Glass House was the job that he gave away!

Olly was nicknamed On It Olly for good reason. When it came to the pitch, he was right on it!

The pitch to Elliott, the IT Director of Maxim Manufacturing had gone well. Reading the body language, voice tone and engagement all the buying signals were good.

Elliott continued to smile and when Olly asked how he was feeling about everything Elliot replied, "Just need to confirm terms and then good to go."

Terms were talked through and then into a recommendation, with three choices for Elliot to choose from. Gold, all singing and dancing, silver mid-way, a popular choice and bronze, a taster to begin working with Elliott.

Olly shared stories about how each recommendation fulfilled the gaps, solved Maxim's IT problems and importantly how chilled Elliott would be when all the updates and tech were installed. His close was, "Shall we begin running the gold-level dark web check or the silver next week? "

Then nothing, total silence. Olly kept his head down looking at his computer, saying nothing. He knew how this worked; he was chilled.

Elliott was thinking, gathering his thoughts which happened more now that he was over 40! He liked Elliott and the recommendations he delivered that seemed to solve many problems. If he went gold the investment was sizeable but good value, whereas silver fitted the budget better. Elliot looked up. "Let's go silver from next week, please!"

Olly smiled. Silver was the middle ground, always a popular choice. Olly relaxed in his chair, suggested a further brew and pulled out his consolidation checklist.

Olly chatted with Elliott, thanking him for his business, talking through what would happen next, who would be in touch, and what was required along with reassurance everything would be put in writing. Olly scheduled his next visit to Maxim, agreed to bring more Jaffa cakes and drank his cup of tea. He was going to enjoy working with Elliott.

As he was packing up, he turned and said, "Just one more thing! I'm looking forward to working with you Elliott. You're switched on and see the value in quality tech and protecting your systems. Who else is like you that I should be arranging to have a coffee with to talk Tech?" Elliott thought for a minute and mentioned Mark from Sky Walk, "I'll text you his number after I've talked to him next week."

Olly headed back to HQ with another deal done, another sale in the bag. It had taken time, but it worked by just following the process and being liked and he won a future referral as well.

Olly knew why he was known as On It Olly - because he was!

33 Step 10, Consolidate

Where the relationship begins!

Step 9 is frequently where most sales processes stop. Oh dear, a missed opportunity. Step 10 Consolidate is where the relationship begins.

I often share the story about Trainee Trevor. Back in the late 1980s, Trevor worked for the local newspaper. His area was North Oxford and included Banbury and Bicester. Trevor enjoyed his job, meeting retailers and designing adverts to feature on the front of this week's local paper. However, Trevor was missing a trick as each week he would begin with no money in "pre-booked" towards his target.

Trevor sold for today, would pop in for a chat and ask if they wanted one ad for that week. Often, they said yes, sometimes no, and for Trevor, it was a numbers game. When he got a yes, he would run out of the store, an advert in hand and head to his big white Maestro with its go-faster stripe. Lighting up a cigarette he would inhale before dialling on his very large mobile. Calling the office with the figures and space sold, then back to his next store as he needed to make his numbers for the week.

Trevor's approach to selling was transactional, one-off with absolutely no client relationship. He did not stick around once a yes was received.

Pre-book was key to hitting the target at the newspaper. Selling campaigns, three, six or twelve months at a time. Up-sell and cross-sell followed if you knew and had a relationship with the customer. Trevor failed and rarely hit the target. He was making life hard for himself. Sales reps often do, only thinking, for now, the short term.

When a yes is received, that desire to celebrate, do a winner's dance and do a mini fist pump is immense. But wait! Thank your new client for their business, suggest they put the kettle on for a second brew and talk through what happens next.

Being detailed now will help alleviate cognitive dissonance or as it is commonly known, buyer's remorse, which is due to land in three days. If you have talked through the next steps, terms, contact info, process, detail, contracts, forms, and payment and importantly have set a date for your next call or visit then you are off to a good start. Asking your new client how many contacts they would like, introducing them to the team, inviting them to see your offices, all this is consolidation. It matters if you are to lock in your customer for the long term.

Having a consolidation checklist is a good idea. It ensures everyone is remembering to stick around and begin what could be a fruitful and trusted relationship. Miss this part and you're heading to a transactional interaction. Such a pity as relationships deliver step 11, the final step - a referral!

34 Step 11, Referral

Referral - the quickest route to a sale.

Step 11 of the selling process is where great prospecting begins. The referral!

Previous chapters share the importance of being referable to be referred and are worth rereading.

The sales process, all steps so nearly complete. The relationship is beginning to bloom, your consolidation is a key part and now you are faced with an opportunity.

Many omit step 11 and move on and out. Often debate is created around the timing of this step. Simply, ask and you will receive, don't and nothing happens. Of utmost importance is timing and how you ask.

Time spent with the prospect who has chosen to become your client has paid off. You are excited about helping solve their problems and create opportunities for their business. They are excited because they have found you and are looking forward to you solving their problems and creating opportunities. So how to fit in a referral, step 11.

Previous chapters looked at the importance of being referable and the value of asking. You understand that to be referred you need to be referable. This is potentially the beginning of a valuable relationship with your new client and jumping right in to ask for a referral requires tact and diplomacy. What you absolutely do not want to do is make them feel like yesterday's news.

Step 11 might fall at the end of a call or in isolation in a future call. What matters is its existence, that it is asked for. When celebrating the future a mention of "we love working with forward-thinking directors like yourself, if there are others in your network who you think might like a call please send them my way."

When asking for referrals, do it in the right way, be thoughtful and recognise timing. Building relationships takes time, years sometimes, but it will be fruitful if you continue to deliver remarkable service. Often when your customers recognise that you're looking to grow, they will happily help and refer you. If they don't know however then they probably won't rush to help fill your pipeline.

Over-eagerness for referrals sends a bad message. It implies that, rather than appreciating their custom you are eager to move on to the next. Who recommends a business like that? So before you raise the prospect of bringing other customers into the relationship, be sure your customer feels special and valued.

In future calls maybe a conversation that looks like this, "Please can you help me, Bill? We are looking to grow with quality organisations, like yours, that value the importance of quality support. Who else in your established network should I be speaking with?" Or "We are looking to grow and have a superb future supporting prestigious companies but are keen to work with forward-thinking manufacturers like yours, that recognise the benefit of quality support. Who else should I be speaking to within your network ?"

It might feel uncomfortable or even strange. But if you are excelling at delivering a superb customer experience and have begun a fruitful relationship then asking for a referral is a fast route to a future sale.

The best referrals look like Wildings Tea Room in Pateley Bridge, in Nidderdale, North Yorkshire.

In Pateley, at the bottom of the High Street is Wildings Tea Room. It looks like most tourist spot cafes: cute tables, laminated menus and a stunning view across the river. This tea room however is sensational, and spectacular and serves up the most delicious, huge, tasty cakes. The scones, tea cakes and lunches are all a delight. But the coffee, now that is special.

There comes an age when good coffee is a must in the day, usually about mid-morning. Instant coffee is ignored and a desire for really good, freshly ground coffee. Personally Taylors Lazy Sunday, made in a cafetière, left for a time added to milk and put into a warmed mug. This coffee with dark chocolate is an everyday luxury. One day we were heading to Pateley. The recommendation was to visit Wildings because the coffee and cake were superb. Begrudgingly and with a thermos cup of my usual coffee in the car, just in case, we headed into Nidderdale.

Leaving the backup coffee in the car we walked, shopped and then went for coffee. My expectations were really low. The cakes, however, did look delicious, with big slices and fabulous flavours, who knew Earl Grey and orange was a thing? Apple, caramel and cinnamon was a great choice and then the coffee. Simply Wow! Just wow, easily on par with my usual, maybe even better. Wonderful tasty coffee served in a warm mug, a large mug. It had a depth of flavour and smelled as good as it tasted. I was amazed, stunned and surprised! This little tea room in Pateley was worthy of referral.

The owners of Wildings have no clue that I went on to include a picture of their tea room in future training. That everyone who talks to me about coffee, a day out or a treat will be pointed in the direction of Wildings. The experience on that morning, our first visit, was so good I became one of their sales force, they just don't know it.

When you delight clients with a phenomenal experience the referrals can follow without prompt. This is a wonderful and fruitful way to receive sales opportunities, it does not just happen. Delivering an unsurpassable customer experience consistently helps to fill your prospecting pipeline with referrals. Referrals lead to sales. Bring solutions and opportunities to new clients and deliver extraordinary to be referred. See how the cycle works?

SUMMARY: MAKE IT LIVE.

Congratulations, you have completed the book, now what? To make it live, to deliver yourself a clear return on investment keep the book out and front of mind.

Sharing knowledge acquired over 30 plus years and relevant training tips on how to sell sincerely has been a pleasure. Initially unsure how the format looked. now it is clear.

Selling begins with mindset. However slick your sales process or prospecting tools, if your mindset is out of kilter, then you will fail.

Understand that feeding your brain the good stuff, and applying grit, graft and tenacity is a "must-have" approach of all great salespeople. Sales will not fall from the air into your lap and nor will you smile once and receive the order. Sales as a career are brilliant, building your network is a pleasure and enhancing your skill set is worthwhile. Make no mistake, selling might look glamorous but behind truly brilliant salespeople is a skill set that is driven by a focused positive mindset and hard work over years.

Understand that you drive your day; planning your time, investing in your education on your topic, taking risks, standing out and approaching your sales role with a plan will work. Understand the critical importance of people

buying people and being able and driven to nurture and cement sincere relationships. Recognise you have just one chance to make a first impression, so make it count.

Before you look at prospecting, look at yourself. Are you coming to this role with a winning mindset? If so, let's prospect.

Remember to profile your ideal client. Being busy in meetings with people who will never spend is time wasted and unlikely to see you achieve your target.

Prospecting, hunting, and failing to be a machine at finding opportunity is where many sales careers falter. The expectation that the phone will ring with people wanting to spend, is swiftly replaced with the recognition that prospecting is hard work, really hard work. Putting on your superhero cape and remembering it is business will help. Next picking up the prospecting toolbox and using all the tools, there is no one magic bullet.

Having a plan to use all the tools and ensuring your customer experience delivers referrals is a great beginning. Remembering the ninety-day rule, factoring in your holidays, down days and the events that happen annually will see your strategy roll out beautifully. Bring your fanatical approach and you will succeed.

Then a sales process, a proven sales process that might work the first time or be split over visits. Understanding big fish go slow, so take time, make time. Importantly having structure allows you to be in control and evaluate which steps are good or need work. It also enables you to be professional and structured in your approach. Miss any one step and the opportunity could be missed, follow them all and you will be selling to everyone!

Use your book. Read once, re-read, share, dip in and out and discuss. Make it live, a point of frequent reference and you will sell more and have happier customers.

Let me know how you get on.
Stay fabulous and winning.

Sally

CHARACTER LIST.

Here is a cast of business people that you will recognise, characters you meet in business and in this book.

Toby is the cynic in the room. Throughout the book, he asks welcome questions that you might relate to.

Wing It Wayne is a salesperson who frequently gets it wrong and On It Olly, his polar opposite, excels in his sales roles.

Other sales characters are:

Bee Gee's Bill is an old-school sales rep. When his sales figures slumped, then Bee Gee's music seemed to help him regain his total of the top biller.

Trainee Trev is brand new to a sales role and eager to learn.

Busy Bella was brilliant at new business development, often referred to as a hunting machine.

Conscientious Colin was superb at delighting customers and winning referral opportunities, but rarely did he focus on new business.

Talkative Tim is a self self-taught salesperson who believed if he talked about his company long enough, the prospect would buy.

Luddite Larry is an old-school sales rep, in post for over 17 years and has absolutely no interest in changing how he does business.

Proactive Piers worked with Larry and he won a new business opportunity using social media.

Every Excuse Ed - underperforming in his sales role and happy to use every excuse as a reason why it was absolutely not his fault.

Fanatical Freya was all over prospecting activity, proud of a winning mindset that consistently created opportunity.

Business Leaders include:

Dynamic Doug, a business leader in London and Brilliant Brenda his trusted receptionist.

Dr Wong of Steve & Co Dental Practice and Ethel the gatekeeper. She is also a Grandma and a trusted influencer.

Characters who network:

Sensational Sunny - networked brilliantly

Tarquin was "up 'issen" when networking

Amy & Annabel - new to a law firm and networking

Stella is an experienced networker who forgot her business cards

Boris is a networker who believes everyone should know who he is

Fred owns a fridge company and loves sharing info about himself. Also writes very long emails

Other characters include

Sighing Sandra, she surrounded herself with negativity and found reason to complain about pretty much everything.

Stacey worked at the Very Big Supermarket and Morris was her customer

No Norman worked in finance at Proctor & Porridge and said "No" to pretty much everything

Yes Sam worked with Norman and was his polar opposite, always saying "Yes"

Ready To Buy Rachel met Bella and was nearly ready to buy what Bella sold.

Richard, my first crush. Rachel, Richard's first crush. George Michael, Rachel's first crush.

Tim Hardy is a superb photographer who is easy to refer as is Paul Webster a superb bank manager.

Alex & Amy, friends who came over for a BBQ. Turns out Amy is vegetarian.

ABOUT THE AUTHOR

Sally Roberts

Sally Roberts is an extraordinary sales trainer. Successful Selling and Customer Experience are what Sally knows best!

Her knowledge of every part of the sales process, mindset, prospecting and selling combined with her inspirational approach to sharing knowledge has meant every business she works with has experienced significant growth. Sally is a trainer who talks the talk and walks the walk. She has worn the T-shirt since the 1980s, selling everything from TVs to radio advertising campaigns. More recently she has established her own highly successful training company. Sally brings positivity and trains hands-on. She will pick up the phone and cold call with you, she will join you at an exhibition or a face to face at a meeting. Sally understands how to sell today, right now and crucially, how to find prospects to sell to.

Sally's style and approach are unique, and exciting and deliver results. Sally creates character-driven stories that you can relate to and remember. She offers pointers and tips that you can use immediately and suggests proven methods for adopting a positive sales mindset, effective prospecting and successful selling. She challenges you to look at every part of your business, to identify where sales opportunities might be created and to jump right on it. She inspires you to try new ways of prospecting, to mix up the tools you have. Most importantly when you create opportunity, Sally shares a proven sales process that will see your sales figures soar. Her #sallyfact videos see her ranking on YouTube.

Eight years ago Sally attended a very expensive sales training course. It was dull, it was a classroom, it was long and boring and it simply did not work. This inspired Sally to walk away from the safety of employment and establish Fun Training For Results, specialising in sales and customer experience.

Her relatable approach to salespeople of all ages and experience sees her recommended by many respected business leaders. Sally's style of training is unique, engaging and fun, as is her debut long-awaited book.

To see more of Sally join her on LinkedIn or check out her #sallyfact videos on sallyfact.co.uk

Printed in Great Britain
by Amazon